CHANGE

YOUR

CLOTHES,

CHANGE

YOUR

LIFE

G

gallery books

new york

london

toronto

sydney

new delhi

CHANGE YOUR CLOTHES,

CHANGE YOUR LIFE

because you can't go naked

GEORGE BRESCIA

Gallery Books
A Division of Simon & Schuster, Inc.
1230 Avenue of the Americas
New York, NY 10020

First Gallery Books hardcover edition August 2014

GALLERY BOOKS and colophon are registered trademarks of Simon & Schuster,
Inc.

For information about special discounts for bulk purchases, please contact Simon &
Schuster Special Sales at 1-866-506-1949 or business@simonandschuster.com.

The Simon & Schuster Speakers Bureau can bring authors to your live event. For
more information or to book an event contact the Simon & Schuster Speakers Bureau
at 1-866-248-3049 or visit our website at www.simonspeakers.com.

Interior design by Jaime Putorti
Cover design by John Vairo
Cover image by Shutterstock
Illustrations by Pat Chang
Author photo by Nina Duncan

Manufactured in the United States of America

10   9   8   7   6   5   4   3   2   1

Library of Congress Cataloging-in-Publication Data
Brescia, George.
  Change your clothes, change your life: because you can't go naked / George Brescia.
    pages cm
  1. Fashion. 2. Women's clothing. 3. Beauty, Personal. I. Title.
  TT507.B674 2014
  646.4'04—dc23

                                        2013040733

ISBN 978-1-4767-4873-3
ISBN 978-1-4767-4876-4 (ebook)

This book is dedicated to _you_, dear reader,
for being brave enough to open your heart,
mind, and closet to change.

CHANGE

YOUR

CLOTHES,

CHANGE

YOUR

LIFE

introduction
a great outfit can change your life

This is not a book about style or fashion.

I repeat: This is not a book about style or fashion.

This is a book about learning to see. It's a book about your relationship to the outside world. About bringing order and harmony to your external appearance, and thus to your inner life. This is a book about how we get in our own way. This is a book about turning up the volume, and living every day to its fullest. This is a book about change.

You *will* learn rules, tips, and shortcuts. You *will* learn about what colors suit you. But you don't need to be interested in style to read this book—in fact, the less interested in style you are, the more you need this book. For style is not the end in and of itself but is instead the gateway to the change you seek. It *is* possible to change your life through your clothes.

If that sounds very far away from where you are now, know that though the transformation you are about to go through is likely to be profound, it will be accomplished via a series of small shifts—shifts that will bear fruit right away. I can say this because I've seen their immediate, life-altering impact over and over and over again.

The immediacy of that impact is one of the things I love most about my work as a stylist—my ability to tangibly change the way a person is perceived, and thus to alter their basic experience of their life, in a single afternoon. It's powerful stuff. One client's mother told me with tears in her eyes that she and her husband had been waiting for me their entire lives: Their daughter was finally dressed like the beautiful woman they knew her to be. Another client who'd radically swapped out her color palette reported an immediate sea change in her coworkers' responses—an uptick in smiles, hellos, and friendly chitchat. Walking around her neighborhood on the weekends felt completely different. The normally surly shopkeeper at her local wine store put down his ledger to tell her that she looked different in a way he couldn't put his finger on. That her *face* looked amazing.

I've seen the transformative powers of great clothing reach far beyond the work of a single day or week or month. Take Jeanne, a single girl when we met, dressing in clothes that weren't right for her body, didn't speak to her professional accomplishments as a highly respected public relations executive, and certainly weren't doing her any favors in the husband-hunting department. In the year we worked together, she met and married the love of her life. They were introduced at a party for which I'd dressed her in a red silk strappy dress and a heap of gold accessories, a perfect example of a woman dressing to be noticed and reaping the benefits. She wasn't the first woman I've seen enact a radical life change that started in her closet, and she won't be the last.

A Great Outfit Can Change Your Life

You already know the power of a great outfit—every woman does. You walk out the door and it just feels *right*. You don't necessarily spend the rest of the day mirror-gazing or snapping selfies or even really thinking about what you're wearing—you simply go about your business feeling better in your skin, with an extra bounce in your step, and others take notice. You're not sure whether it's that extra bit of confidence or whether the universe is smiling back at you, but the day somehow just seems to go . . . better.

The proof is in your gut, but the science backs it up: Studies show that people considered attractive have better chances of nailing the job interview, snagging those airline upgrades, or getting seated at the best table in the house. Scientists tend to focus on facial symmetry and that ineffable quality known as "beauty"—but what they ignore is the extent to which your clothing can *draw out* your natural beauty, and thus significantly affect the outcome of your days.

That—and much more—is the power of great style.

My ultimate goal in this book is for you to have the feeling that comes with an indisputably great outfit, that bounce in your step, and that feeling of easy confidence, every day; to be able to open the door to your closet with a buoyant sense of expectation, rather than a feeling of dread. And then to step out your front door feeling like you can conquer the world. The net result will be a change in mind-set with ramifications that will spiral out into every area of your life.

The Language of Style

Though I see all kinds of clients, I work with a number of stage actresses. I've found this work to be extremely relevant to everything I do, because it brings up *so* many questions about perception. When an actress calls me for help dressing for an audition, we think beyond just getting her to look gorgeous. We think about the role she's going in for and how that translates into her clothes. Maybe she needs to look like a publisher. What does a publisher look like? Maybe she needs to look like a lawyer from Milwaukee who has two kids and is coming off the baseball field to go meet a client. How do we use clothing to convey these very subtle distinctions?

For me, style is a language, and it all comes down to a series of messages—messages that are constantly being decoded by the people we cross in our daily lives. In this book, I am going to teach you not only how to overhaul your wardrobe so that you look your very best, but also how to decode and recalibrate these messages so that *you* can begin to take full and total control of the impressions you are creating.

Talk to Me

As you are probably beginning to sense, my end goal here goes far beyond getting you into a cute outfit.

Ultimately, I want *you* to hone your fashion IQ, to become fluent with the tools that I use in my work so that you can employ them on your own. But because I won't be there to give you the face-to-face feedback I give my clients, I want to encourage you to reach out to me in whatever way works best for you. On Twitter, I'm @georgebstyle. You can find me on Facebook, or you can email me at georgebstyleny@gmail.com. If you reach out, I *will* answer—because I honor your commitment to this process, and I understand that at times you will need support. So tweet me a pic of that outfit you're unsure of. Send me the style questions that have you totally flummoxed. Let me know how this process is going for you. I want to be by your side as you embark on this most personal and rewarding of transformations.

I can't wait to see the results.

chapter 1

the secret language of clothing
learning to read your wardrobe

Style is a simple way of saying complicated things.
—Jean Cocteau

Whether your starting point is a full-blown style crisis or just a sense that your current wardrobe is in need of improvement, if you've picked up this book, you're looking for change. Maybe clothing has been a lifelong struggle and you've finally decided to tackle the issue head-on. Maybe you're contemplating a career or personal transition that has you anxious to put your best foot forward, but unsure of how to do it. Or maybe you've always wondered what it would be like to have a personal stylist of your very own.

Whatever your reasons, I'm glad you are here. Welcome to the world of George B Style!

For me, clothing is nothing but pure fun, but I've seen firsthand how very much my clients struggle with style, how fraught and emotional and personal and *deep* this subject can be. Yet so often, style is treated as though it's a problem with a simple solution: a formulaic makeover with a side of increased consumption.

The idea that you can simply buy your way to a better closet is highly flawed. While I do believe there are certain core elements every woman needs in a fully functioning wardrobe, it is also my belief that most style problems start on the inside. They start with long-held beliefs about our limitations, whether physical or mental. They start with fear—whether it's a fear of being seen, a fear of being ignored, or a fear of change, aging, progress, and responsibility. They start with confusion about their identities and the various roles they play in their lives.

Why is clothing so emotional, and for many of us, so fraught? Well, first off, clothing is what literally keeps us from going naked. It is a second skin, and its proximity to our actual skin cannot help but bring up a wealth of emotions surrounding body image, self-worth, confidence, and identity. In a very real way, it hides our most vulnerable selves.

It is the bridge between our private, interior worlds and the public, external world through which we travel.

It is a shape-shifting cloak with a symbolic power that works in two ways: deeply affecting our sense of self while simultaneously informing the perceptions of strangers, acquaintances, and loved ones alike. Clothing, more than any of our possessions, has the power to define our identity.

Your Style Is Speaking *for* You

Here is the central truth of this book: *Our clothes speak for us before we do.*

Countless studies have proven the sway that first impressions have over our perceptions of the people we come into contact with every day—and over their perceptions of us. Within ten seconds of a first meeting, an impression is formed, and an opinion begins to coalesce.

Think about it: In your daily life, how often do you make assumptions about the people you come across? You spot a man in his mid-forties in the checkout line at your neighborhood grocery store. I can guarantee you that in a matter of seconds, you have taken in enough about his clothing, hair, and general appearance to process guesses as to what he does for a living, how much money he makes, how much you might or might not have in common, and maybe even his politics. These guesses go *way* beyond the difference between a construction worker in paint-spattered work boots and a banker in a manicured Brooks Brothers suit—our eyes are extremely discerning, quickly taking in very subtle details. If he's wearing jeans, it doesn't take a professional stylist to make a snap judgment as to what those jeans *mean*. You do it all the time, whether you're conscious of it or not. Are they beat-up dungarees that have seen their fair share of drywall, or carefully distressed artisan denim with a price tag north of $150? What does the style of the jean, the hair, the shirt, and the shoe *say*? "Architect" or "entertainment lawyer"? Serious and ambitious, or laid-back and fun-loving? Possible future husband or commitment-phobe with a Peter Pan complex? Your brain is constantly collecting visual clues and arranging them into patterns—patterns that turn into assumptions.

And here's the rub: The same thing is happening to you, *every time you step outside your home*. The outfit you casually threw on in an early morning haze? It's being assessed by strangers and acquaintances alike as a clue to your character, your identity, and your overall appeal.

That's why I believe that *everything* we put on our bodies is a "statement piece," whether we're talking about the ten-year-old sweats and scary flip-flops you threw on for a grocery store run or the drab office uniform you haven't tweaked since *Designing Women* was still on the air.

You're probably familiar with the concept of the statement piece. The term sprouts up all over the place in fashion magazines and on makeover shows—it's stylist code for an eye-catching, colorful garment or accessory that defines your entire look in one fell swoop. But if you think about clothing through the lens of that ten-second rule, you'll come to realize that there is no such thing as a non-statement piece.

Everything we wear makes some kind of a statement, whether it's a dull army-green puffy coat paired with faded black khakis or a great-fitting pair of jeans flanked by a crisp white tee and a classic navy blazer.

Whether we like it or not, we are being seen. Our statement is being deciphered. And the reach of that statement goes far, far beyond the fleeting impression of a stranger on the checkout line.

Learning to "Read" Your Own Statement

Here's the good news: Your clothing may be speaking volumes, but what it *doesn't* have is a mind of its own. That is to say, your outfit didn't simply slip off of its hanger and fling itself onto your body—somebody selected it for you, and that somebody (YOU!) can choose to make different decisions, more educated decisions, more conscious decisions. Better decisions. *You* have the power to change your statement, and it's a change whose effects will ricochet throughout your entire life.

But before you can tweak the statement your clothing is making, you're going to need to learn to read it. Learn to decipher the statements your clothing is making and you will know exactly how to dress.

It starts with a very simple shift: paying attention. If there's one activity you are going to hear me endorse again and again, it is being more attentive—for it is my sincere belief that the difference between a fantastic outfit and a not-so-great one is largely a matter of consciousness. Ask any guru, philosopher, or psychologist and they'll tell you that real change begins with mindfulness—which is just a fancy word for paying attention and being present to your life.

Where do I get off making it sound as though if you simply get in touch with your third eye, you'll instantly morph into a modern-day version of Jackie Onassis? Because I know that every woman has the ability to piece together a great outfit, a skill she tends to demonstrate when the stakes are high or when the event requires it. Think of the last time you went on a job interview or attended a wedding. Whether you shopped for the occasion or simply pulled that go-to power outfit out of your closet, I'm quite certain you turned up in something that showcased the best of your style, figure, and personality.

Your proven ability to turn up the heat, using nothing more than a little forethought and some extra effort, proves my point: When we pay attention to what we are wearing, to the statement we are making, our outfits wind up telling a different story. A much, much better story.

On some level, the greatest gift I give my clients is my undivided attention. When they work with me, they gain an extra set of eyes that objectively evaluates the statements their outfits are making, urging them not to settle for the ill-fitting, the good-enough, or the timid. If you cultivate your awareness, you will learn to act as this objective witness for yourself—and you will soon hold the key to controlling the story that your clothing tells about you.

Cultivating that awareness begins with a very simple question.

"What Does It Say?"

This is my golden question, the question I want you to ask of every single outfit you put on your body. It's such a simple question, really, but it's one I find to be incredibly powerful. Instead of just throwing outfits together and hoping for the best, you're going to be interrogating your clothing in order to come to a deeper understanding of the statements it is making.

Though it requires a major shift in perception and will eventually entail an entirely new approach to your wardrobe, this process of interrogation will come far more easily than you may imagine.

Think about the speed with which you made those snap judgments about that handsome architect in the grocery store line—one quick look at the cut of his jeans told you so much. Now you will be turning that razor-sharp perceptiveness around and applying it to yourself. If it only takes you ten seconds to "read" the signals put out by strangers you cross on the street, it shouldn't take you much longer to submit your own reflection to the very same scan. When *you* are the stranger in the grocery store line, what are other people seeing?

Does your clothing communicate success, happiness, hopefulness, and confidence, or does it betray insecurity, bashfulness, confusion, and fear? Is it true to the life stage you inhabit or hope to inhabit, or does it speak to a long-gone self of decades past?

If you're looking down at the outfit you have on right now and drawing a blank as to what it communicates, don't worry. Throughout this book, I am going to be teaching you how to evaluate the message of your clothing based on its colors, its overall harmony, and its fit and form. All I am going to ask of you is that every morning as you are getting dressed you begin to pose the golden question—"What does this say?" Eventually, the answers will emerge. And when they do, nothing will stand in your way . . .

the compact of truth

mirror, mirror

There's no getting around it: In order to transform your style and take charge of the messages you're putting out in the world, you're going to have to start spending some serious time in front of your mirror. If you want to gain control over what other people see in you, you must gather all the visual information these strangers and acquaintances have at their disposal. The only way to do that is by taking a good, hard look at yourself in the mirror.

Is this a prospect that fills you with dread? Do you habitually avoid your reflection because you're unhappy with what you see? We bring so many of our hang-ups to that glassy surface, sometimes shunning it like it's our worst enemy. But this is counterproductive—because even if you're not looking, someone else is.

So much of this process is about learning how to *look*. And there's lots to learn by looking at your reflection, beginning with how it makes you feel and ending with what exactly it is that you see. Take inventory—but be nice! That's my girl you're talking about . . .

Your Little Black Book

The first purchase I'm going to ask you to make may take you by surprise. It's not a new bra (though if you've never been fitted, you absolutely *should* make that item number two on your to-do list) or a little black dress. Instead, I'm going to ask you to acquire a brand-new notebook that will be exclusively dedicated to this life-altering endeavor, and to this endeavor only. This little black book—though in fact it may be turquoise, orange, or any color you choose—will be the repository of the various pieces of journaling we're going to be doing throughout this process. Eventually, it will morph into your fashion to-do list, as well as a place to jot down the random inspirations and ideas you come upon as you go through this transformation. If you're so wedded to your devices that you shun the idea of putting pen to paper, a digital version of the little black book is acceptable—but when I'm embarking on a new life stage, I like having a physical object that becomes a tangible touchstone for my process.

Taking Inventory

Put on your favorite body-conscious outfit, the close-fitting, revealing ensemble you feel most attractive in and/or that garners you the most compliments, be it a work outfit, a night-out-on-the-town outfit, or even flattering workout gear. With a handheld mirror at the ready, stand before your full-length mirror. What do you see? Use the handheld mirror to get a full, 360-degree view so that you can check yourself out from the front, the sides, and the back. With your little black book by your side, jot down the answers to the following questions:

- What are your "assets"? What are the defining features of your face and body? What instantly stands out about you and makes you *you*? Your eyes, your hair, your curves, your height, your bone structure, your coloring? Gaining a conscious understanding of which parts of your body to emphasize and reveal can turn zoned-out shopping trips into targeted, goal-oriented missions with infinitely greater chances of success. You'll be able to nix entire categories of clothing at a glance, and you'll have a pretty good shot at knowing what looks good on you before even trying it on.

- What compliments do you regularly receive from your friends? You may be too mired in self-criticism to recognize your best physical attributes, so think about what you hear from the people who love you. Are they always harping on your tiny waist? Jealously eyeing your long legs? Telling you they'd kill for your shoulders? Making lovingly lewd comments about your cleavage? The areas most often complimented are likely to be the ones you'll want to reveal or enhance.

- How does the outfit you have on highlight your assets? You may know what clothing you feel best in, but have you ever analyzed why? Break it down. Is that dress nipped in at the waist? Are those straps the perfect width, giving you a defined shoulder line and appearing to shrink your upper body in half? Does that racerback tank make the most of your beautiful back? Does the color make you pop, drawing out your eyes and giving you a healthy, happy glow? Start to catalog the attributes that make this favorite outfit so great, and you're on your way to becoming a more educated shopper.

- Which assets *aren't* being accentuated by your outfit? Do you have a lovely pair of gams that never see the light of day? Whatever your excuses for hiding them away—"My legs aren't really that great" or "I don't want to look like I'm trying too hard"—set them aside. Jot down a note promising that when we get to Chapter 6, "A Fresh New Start," you are going to purchase at least one thing that accentuates this unrealized asset. You may feel uncomfortable the first time you wear it (more on that later), but my guess is that you will soon be strutting your stuff.

■ What are your "liabilities," those aspects of your appearance you wouldn't rush to show off? I know there's a tendency for you to go to town here, but try not to go off the rails by listing every single part of your body. Keep it positive, and be as kind to yourself as you would be to a good friend. Everyone has flaws, and styling is about downplaying those flaws and highlighting the positives. So think less "I hate my tummy!" and more "My midsection is my problem area, so I'm going to look for clothing that either flows over it or belts me in, giving me structure and the illusion of a waist" or "My arms are not my best feature—so three-quarter sleeves are best for me."

Ninety-nine percent of my clients perceive their bodies so inaccurately that their views of their own flaws are downright comical. I want you to use this exercise to set the record straight. Are your negative misconceptions about your looks so powerful that a pattern of mirror avoidance has set in? Are you afraid of what you might see? Odds are the reality is much, much better than what you're imagining—we are *always* our own worst critics.

The mirror is not your enemy. The mirror is nothing but a tool—a tool that you are going to start using, every single day, to positively skew the balance between those assets and liabilities. To draw the eye to the positives, and away from the negatives. You have so much more power to affect the outcome than you know. But you have to be brave enough to look.

"Tell Me Everything"

"Tell me everything." That's the sentence with which I begin every session with a first-time client, and it's where we're going to start our process as well. Before we get into your closet, we're going to take stock of where you are and start to visualize what it is you want for yourself. Where are you in your life, and where do you want to be? How are your clothes helping you reach this goal? How are they hindering you? You'll discover much, much more as you begin to assess your wardrobe in Chapter 5, but I find it helpful to anchor the process with a focused look at your status and your goals.

In your little black book, write down the answers to the following questions:

- What is the image you currently portray in your professional life? How do you feel about that image? How do you think it hinders or furthers your goals?

- What is your approach to your weekend wardrobe? Are you having fun with your weekend clothes, or do you take more of a cloak-of-invisibility approach?

What is your priority in weekend clothes—practicality, style, flexibility, a combination?

- What kind of occasion causes you the most stress? If you have to pull something together for a cocktail party or a presentation, what are you wearing? What would you like to be wearing?

- Overall, do you think your clothes speak to where you are in your life, and to where you want to be in the next five years?

- How do you wish things were different?

- What are your style struggles? Do you have a hard time finding pants that fit? Love the way you look in a cardigan, not so comfortable in a blazer? Always looking for a way to camouflage your tummy or your thighs? Stuck in clunky shoes because of back problems?

- What do you feel best in? What types of outfits make you feel most yourself—and why?

- How do you *feel* in the clothes you currently wear? Visible? Attractive? Professional? Cheerful? How would you like to feel?

- What does it feel like to confront your closet every day?

- What kind of change are you hoping to enact by going through this process?

This exercise will help you begin to hone your fashion vision. I often find that I learn almost everything I need to know about a client in the course of this initial talk; what we then see in her closet only serves to confirm what she and I already know to be true. It's a pretty profound indication of the fact that, deep down, you already know the strengths and weaknesses of your wardrobe. Articulating this knowledge is half the battle, as it lays the groundwork for the change we seek.

Dress for the Life You Want

"Dress for the job you want, not the job you have." I bring up this bit of motherly counsel because I think it's such great advice, holding at its core a nugget of truth that suggests how much our appearance colors other people's perceptions and judgments. That if we want to succeed in our professional lives, doing a great job isn't enough. We must also communicate a sense of competence, ambition, and poise—messages best transmitted via nonverbal cues, through our clothing, our body language, and our overall charisma.

Deep down, we all understand how critical this dress-as-if directive can be on the job front—even if we sometimes ignore it, especially as we grow more comfortable in our positions. But many of us fail to realize the relevance of this concept to every single space we inhabit or pass through.

Your clothing emits a series of messages that are being perceived and responded to in every area of your life, whether you're at the office or on a bus on your way to Poughkeepsie.

You never know who you're going to run into in these in-between spaces—that lovely and well-connected woman from your book group you've been meaning to call, that not-so-lovely and seriously judgmental woman from your PTA board who sees any sign of weakness as an opportunity for a power grab, or, indeed, that stranger whose acquaintance could change the entire course of your professional or romantic life in one fell swoop.

But dressing for the non event, whether it's a day full of errands or a lazy weekend by the shore, isn't just about being attuned to the impression you are making on others. The messages carried by your clothing don't only travel outward—they also boomerang their way back to you, affecting your deepest sense of self and identity. They color the stories you tell yourself about the world and your place in it.

When we're dressed more professionally, we *feel* more professional. When we're dressed to seduce, we *feel* more seductive. When we're dressed more festively, we *feel* more festive. Add your own adjective, and continue down the line. . . . Crisp, fresh, interesting, intellectual, powerful, approachable, cheerful, sophisticated, playful, serious, pretty, expensive—or on the flip side, dowdy, messy, bland, confusing, mismatched, threadbare, cheap. Whatever its content, the message your clothing communicates to the outside world is also internalized by its first and most important witness: you.

What does *feeling* more professional, more sophisticated, more powerful, or more seductive have to do with *becoming* all those things?

Everything.

Nothing affects the course of our lives so much as the state of our minds. But many of us neglect the key role our clothing can take in changing our mind-sets.

So what would it look like to dress for the life you want? What is it that you want more of in your life? Adventure, relaxation, professional recognition, romance, fun? Are you dressing to reap these possibilities, or to turn them away?

Dress to Be Seen—And to Be Seen at Your Best

Cassie, a Broadway performer and one of my dearest clients, is a five-foot-ten redhead with legs up to her ears, a voice like butter, and the classic features of a 1940s movie star. Just your average, drop-dead gorgeous pinup. The hitch? She doesn't like being tall.

Or at least didn't before I got to her. Didn't like standing out in a crowd, didn't want to draw "too much attention" to herself, and dressed in a sad mix of oh-so-blah twinsets and prim high-necked blouses that ensured she would slide into invisibility every time she stepped off the stage.

Rewind. An actress who doesn't care for attention? Perhaps it would be more accurate to say that, given her naturally high level of visibility as both a tall woman and a redhead, she was afraid of attracting the *wrong kind* of attention—and I don't mean in a "girl from the wrong side of the tracks" sort of way. If you're unsure about your fashion choices, attention can be scary. You exist in a permanent "Don't look at me because I'm not really sure how good this looks!" mode.

I'm not going to lie—this is a woman who was basically a stylist's dream. Once we got her into some clothes she could feel 100 percent confident about, the transformation was pretty radical. I gave her the tools she needed to feel good about her appearance, and she began giving herself permission to be as tall and statuesque as she really was, eventually embracing her height as an asset. It was a revelation. "My whole life is different," she told me. "Now I go to these events and everyone freaks out over how great I look, where before I felt like people didn't really notice me."

What was her prescription for star quality? It started with recalibrating the palette of her wardrobe around her ivory skin and her shock of red hair, reorienting her toward those colors that flattered her natural hues— creams, blues, greens, the *right* reds, camels, and golds. It started with taking advantage of the physical attributes she had previously been downplaying. Pouring her into dresses that fit her like a glove, even getting her to step out in a hot pant and a heel to show the world those beautiful legs. Turning up the heat in a major way, and giving her permission to be the glamour girl that she'd always secretly wanted to be.

Now she's considered one of the best-dressed people on Broadway, and she divides her life into pre- and post-George eras.

Granted, most of us don't spend our nights posing under the glare of a photographer's lights or signing autographs on our way home from work. But Cassie's story does illustrate some points that apply to everyone. First and foremost, that even those women who seem to have it all (the height, the gams, the dewy, dewy skin) share the same hang-ups and uncertainties as the rest of us—they find fault where there is none, or feel self-conscious about those qualities that actually make them unique. That we are all, at times, so confounded by the rules of style that instead of facing them head-on, we turn tail and run away. We know we're not getting it right, and so we choose to hide, camouflaging not only our flaws but also our greatest assets.

So many of the most common style mistakes come out of the urge to hide. The dull palettes, the oversize sacks, the unflinching adherence to a uniform of notice-me-not "basics," day after day after day. (Yes, old gray slacks, tired blue button-down, threadbare beige cardigan, I am talking to you . . .) That schoolgirl scurrying down the hall, head pitched down and books clutched to her chest, is only rendered more noticeable by her ardent wish for invisibility. Hiding doesn't relieve us of the gaze of others—it only highlights our discomfort and awkwardness, making *those* our most visible qualities.

I cannot stress how important it is for you to accept your visibility. *Embrace* your height, your curves, your coloring, whatever it is that makes you look like you and makes you stand out from the crowd. Dress to highlight your assets. Because if you dress to be seen, you will automatically be dressing to be seen at your best.

Dress to Win

Why do politicians agonize for hours over the shirt-and-tie combinations they wear to their debates? Why is there an entire organization—the charity called Dress for Success—

devoted to helping underprivileged women transform their professional lives by overhauling their wardrobes?

Because in the game of life, success is predicated on self-presentation. Because appearance determines our fate.

Honey, I can hear your moans and groans loud and clear. I see your resistance to this seemingly superficial state of affairs on a daily basis. You know who you are—you may not be fully conscious of it, but on some level you've opted to check out of the game by wearing dull or ill-fitting clothes that telegraph your low opinion of the status quo. (Though maybe deep down you secretly love to shop and stockpile a closetful of pretty things you feel too guilty to wear.)

If you are consciously or subconsciously engaging in a form of sartorial rebellion, please, please ask yourself what you stand to gain. Clothing that issues statements such as "I don't care what you think" or "I'd rather you not see me at all" is surprisingly effective at alienating people and sabotaging interactions.

Is our image-conscious status quo really such a terrible thing? I don't think so. Our sensitivity to appearances, our attraction to the visual, isn't so much the result of a mean-spirited shallowness as it is the direct product of our biology. The eye prefers harmony to chaos. Why? Because visual chaos engages the brain in a game of "What the heck is going on here/is a baboon about to eat me?" Given how high a degree of competition there is for our attention these days, the ensemble that produces such an emotion is likely to be willfully tuned out. (Or perhaps it will be inspected, but to the detriment of its wearer.)

Yes, there is an element of artifice in all of this. We're going to be honing and then using our visual intelligence to affect the way others perceive us. But here's the thing: If it's all a game, why not dress to win? You're playing, whether you realize it or not.

How You Do Anything Is How You Do Everything

The story your clothing is telling is only the beginning. Cultivating awareness and learning to pay attention matter not *just* because of the material results they enable, but also because of what these habits of mind signify in the larger scheme of our lives. What else are you ignoring? Your finances? Your friendships? Your health? I don't know about you, but I tend to ignore those things I fear, those parts of my life that fill me with uncertainty, anxiety, and dread. Bad idea. When we let fear rule our actions (or lack thereof), the results are never pretty. A pattern of *inattention* can be just as impactful, in the negative sense, as calculated *intention* can be in the positive.

This is obviously true for your wardrobe—a wardrobe built out of fear and inattention will almost certainly be subpar. But because one black hole creates another, you cannot simply close the door to that hot mess of a closet of yours and dwell in the rest of your life without consequences. Or, to put it another way: *How you do anything is how you do everything.* Think of the care with which a traditional Japanese tea is served, the ceremony with which a kimono is slipped on. Why do the Japanese take such care with their rituals? To cultivate an unbroken sense of grace that extends out from the action to every area of life. Similarly, you can use fashion to become present in your life.

Soon, you will be making conscious decisions about everything you put on your body, and the way in which every piece comes together into a whole picture, every single day. That care will affect the perceptions of every single person with whom you interact, thus shaping your fate in incalculable ways.

Life Is Not a Series of Events

If you're thinking, *Enough already with this awareness/ consciousness jibber-jabber, I thought I was reading a book about fashion!*, let me put it to you in yet another way: For most of us, real life is not a series of events calling for cocktail dresses, "day-to-night" outfits, or impeccably pressed suits. The average day is generally, well, average, sometimes containing no more exotic a medley than running errands, ferrying children to and fro, making dinner, doing the dishes, tidying up, and, at some point, collapsing in an exhausted heap. But that doesn't mean there's no room for a harmonious and flattering outfit that helps you make the best of your day.

Beyond that, when you dress only for the events you know about, you are missing out on the chance to seize the opportunities you *didn't* know were there. Wouldn't you rather start from a place that has you treating every day as an unknown quantity, full of potential surprises?

Here's the mind-set from which I operate: I believe that the world is essentially a small town in which you never know who you're going to run into, and what role that person may come to play in your life. The fact that I live in New York, the biggest small town this side of Paris, may have something to do with that—our sidewalks boast a heady mix of opportunity, pedestrian traffic, and high fashion. But I'd live by this rule in Tulsa, Dubuque, and Wichita, too. I don't want to exist in a world in which I wake up and expect that nothing exciting is going to come out of my day! So I always dress as if I might turn a corner and run into my next client, my next best friend, my next big adventure.

What does that mean for a day comprising a session at the gym, a trip to the grocery store, a stop at the dry cleaners? For me, probably a stellar pair of dark jeans, a clean and fresh (that is, not faded or holey) tee, and my cherry-red, twenty-dollar zip-up hoodie. Sounds like a stylist's dream, right? I'm the first to admit it's nothing special. But it's all about that bright red hoodie. I could have worn a gray hoodie—but with a pair of jeans and a tee, what does that outfit say? *Don't look at me,* or, *I expect nothing out of this day.* A pop of color changes all of that. Not just any color, of course, but a color that happens to look great on me, that works with and not against my hair color, my skin tone, and my eyes. All of a sudden, I'm noticeable. I'm playful. I'm cheerful. And I'm brave. That twenty-dollar sweatshirt changes everything. And it doesn't take a whole lot of forethought. Because my closet is filled with clothing that flatters me and that projects a range of positive statements from the casually cheerful to the powerfully tailored, even when I'm rushed and grabbing for something easy and last-minute, I'm never in danger of dressing for a drab, fruitless day.

By the end of this book, you'll be able to say the same. But somewhere along the way, you're going to have to examine your mind-set and make sure that you're open to a shift that's more profound than a superficial makeover. Are you ready to dress for possibility? To prepare yourself, every day, to encounter a matrix of hidden opportunities you don't know about in advance? It's a bit scary, to be sure, in the way that the unknown is always scary. But it's also so exciting.

Rent-a-George

Though I'm going to be by your side throughout this process, it never hurts to have an extra pair of objective eyes on hand. So recruit a friend to be your fashion buddy—we'll call him (or her) Rent-a-George.

Who is the George in your life? Obviously he or she ought to be an incredibly attractive, chic, and intelligent sort, someone with a keen wit, a great sense of style, a kind way with words, and a discerning eye. (If I do say so myself!) Ideally, this is someone who knows you well and with whom you are comfortable. This tends to be a fun project, so I don't imagine you'll have trouble finding a volunteer, especially if he or she has long wanted to see you stretch your style muscles.

The hitch: "George" needs to have read this book, too! So pass him your copy, or better yet, have him buy his own. Like I said, I'm assuming your George will have an impeccable sense of style, but it wouldn't hurt to make sure he's conversant with your colors and understands the deeper nature of this quest.

A very important note: George *cannot* be your mother or your significant other. Those relationships are *much* too freighted with history, expectations, pressure, and mutual projection. We heap enough emotion onto our clothing as it is—you need someone who is going to be able to act as an objective and unemotional second eye. P.S.: Bullies need not apply. Give the job to someone with an honest yet gentle way with words, someone whose opinion you will feel comfortable ignoring if it just doesn't feel right.

Now let the journey begin!

chapter 2
how to get dressed
a radical new way to approach your daily routine

Fashion is architecture: It is a matter of proportions.
—Coco Chanel

Take a moment to consider the general tenor of your morning styling ritual. What does getting dressed look like for you? Is your current routine a mad race against the clock? A near-violent scramble that has you flinging undesirable garments from your drawers in search of that one acceptable top, and ends with an unhappy trail of clothing and shoes strewn across your floor? A chaotic or halfhearted chore in which you struggle just to get to a place that feels "good enough"?

You are certainly not alone. These patterns are huge, and they're clues not only to the well-being of your wardrobe, but also to the mind-set with which you approach that wardrobe. Luckily, you won't need years of therapy to overcome these unhappy circumstances; you will, however, need to make a concerted effort to change your habits.

Before we make over your closet, we're going to reframe the day-to-day method by which you dress—because even a closet filled with the very best pieces will yield poor results if its captain (that's you!) is steering her ship in a manic frenzy. The end point, difficult as it may be to imagine, is a dressing routine that has you luxuriating in your choices. Calmly deliberating about what you wish to project. Adding and subtracting until your reflection has the look of a harmonious painting. And then walking out the door with a spring in your step, rather than starting out the day feeling already defeated and ill-equipped for what's ahead.

A Terrible Outfit Can Ruin Your Entire Day

Let me just begin by saying: *Ugh*.

You know the drill. You start out your morning harried and rushed, or you're just not in the mood to think about what you're going to wear. You shower and grab for whatever is clean and close at hand. And you leave your house in an outfit that you are fully aware isn't great.

Maybe it isn't slimming, maybe it doesn't look put-together, maybe it looks dated, or schlumpy, or strange, or just boring, or all of the above. You didn't feel good about it when you looked in the mirror, but you figured you'd power through anyway. You ran out of time, and you don't have much going on that day anyway—no meetings, no lunch date, no social events, nothing special. And who cares—they're just clothes, right?

But you walk ten steps out the door and instantly regret the choices you made in front of that mirror. You wish you'd thrown those jeans away the last time you went through your closet, because they always, always, always make you feel heavy. You wish you'd switched out the bag you know clashes with your outerwear. You are becoming painfully aware of the fact that you have chosen to wear approximately five colors and three or so patterns. And now you are stuck with those early morning choices for the entire day. You try to go about your business and ignore your discomfort, but it's no use: Your self-consciousness colors your every moment and interaction, and you feel like hiding somewhere out of sight, wearing some kind of an "I know I'm wearing a crappy outfit so please don't look at me and judge" sign.

Am I exaggerating? I don't think so. There really is no understating the effect that a terrible or even not-so-good outfit can have on our mood and our self-confidence. You certainly wouldn't want to run into a person of romantic or professional interest on one of these days. You wouldn't want to cross your worst enemy in an alley, either, I'd bet. Nor would you even willingly run into a casual acquaintance. You'd really prefer not to have to see anyone.

These days don't just happen by accident. Generally, they're the result of that early morning moment when we decide to throw in the towel. And often this really is a conscious decision: I know that many of my clients make a distinction between those days on which they "try" and those days on which they don't. That's the moment I want to reframe for you.

I understand that we have varying levels of energy to devote to our morning routines. But why would you willingly set yourself up for a day in which you are ducking all social interactions? I want so much more than that for you, whether the main public event in your day is your six-year-old's soccer match or a lunchtime dash to the salad bar. That's why one of my biggest goals in this book is to get you to question the assumption that there are certain days on which you should *try* to look great, and other days on which it doesn't matter.

Women with great style don't flip the switch on and off—as you may have noticed, even when they're casual, they somehow manage to look really, really good. Why do they bother paying so much attention? Because they understand what's at stake. And how do they pull off looking so great all the time? Because they practice every day!

These women have what I like to call great "fashion muscles." And because they flex them every day, those muscles never atrophy. In this chapter, we're going to spend some time imagining what it would look like to have *you* flexing yours—yes, every day.

Make Sure It Has Harmony

Many of the women I work with have a misconception about great style. Beyond the fact that they think it's unattainable (which it most certainly is *not*), they assume that style has to do largely with shopping, with having the money, the time, and the know-how to acquire the best of the best. But great style is less about what happens in the dressing room mirror on those sporadic shopping trips and more about what happens in front of *your* mirror, every day.

That is to say: Great style isn't so much about what you buy and what you own, although that will come into play, as it is about how you put it all together in your daily life. While my job as a stylist does involve a fair amount of shopping, it also involves a ton of *styling*.

Outside of a professional context, what does that mean? Styling means looking at the whole picture, and tweaking until it works. When I style a client, I am looking at how each and every piece that goes on my client's body comes together to create an overarching effect. Even when it comes to a dress—a piece of clothing many women consider the end point of an outfit—I consider how the shoes, the outerwear, the scarf, the hair, the makeup, and the bag coalesce around that dress, and even more important, around that particular woman. Add in a consciousness about how the colors, fabrics, textures, patterns, and styles are coming together and you have a recipe for success.

This holistic point of view is totally translatable to a

DIY experience. It all comes down to harmony, which is an incredibly powerful shortcut to great style. The human eye is drawn to harmony, whether in paintings, in our homes, in nature, or in fashion. We love a fluid, unbroken picture in which no piece is disruptive or jarring or confusing—this is what we call beauty. But while we may appreciate its handiwork in the art we enjoy or the landscapes we photograph, most of us overlook its potential role in our wardrobes. And so it is that many of my clients suffer from what I like to call the "Clown College" syndrome. They may have good taste, wearing outfits in which each individual piece makes some kind of aesthetic sense, but when it comes to the details or the way it comes together, they let the picture fall apart. They are paying attention to the shopping, not so much to the dressing.

How do you know if your outfit has harmony? You have only to *look*. Does every piece make sense as part of the whole? Or have you tossed a chunky gold and orange scarf knit by a friend (contributing two colors *and* a rough-hewn texture that reads as a pattern) over a black and white flower-printed dress (two other colors and yet another pattern), and topped it with a ribbed brown cardigan (more color and texture), black tights, and a pair of heavily detailed cowboy boots? Congratulations, for you are a graduate of Clown College! Such an ensemble is not terribly unusual, nor is it outwardly offensive. But here's what it does: It distracts. It draws the focus to that incongruous scarf rather than to the face artfully framed by a lovely neckline and adorned with a delicate swath of white silk. It attracts attention to the clunky brown boots that truncate the leg when placed beside the black tights. It confuses the eye.

And when we see an outfit that is confusing, our eyes and our brains register both the outfit and its owner as visual noise. Think of what happens when you hear a grating, cacophonous piece of music. Do you tune in to try to understand it? Maybe, if you are trying to impress a date at a "new jazz" concert in some tiny, hole-in-the-wall bar. But as you're going about your daily life, the likeliest answer is that you tune it out.

To be tuned out is the last thing I want for you.

Make the Mirror Your Friend

In order to understand whether your outfits have harmony, you're going to have to spend a lot more time looking at them. That perfunctory glance to which you may be accustomed will itself undergo a makeover. Because you're not just going to be looking in the mirror at your shirt and pants to make sure you're not too bloated for that combination today. You're going to give your outfits a second and third glance, to make sure that the shoes and jewelry you add work as well, and then a final look to ensure that your choices of outerwear and bag are working together toward a harmonious whole.

Gazing upon your reflection isn't a form of narcissism—it's a form of honesty, a tool that you must become comfortable with if you are going to cultivate your vision. Spending extra time in the mirror may feel odd at first, but it will become easier over time. If you find yourself tearing your reflection to bits, remember that you're not going for perfection—there is no such thing. Your aim is *harmony*, something anyone can attain. And though you want to activate an awareness that encompasses both your assets and your liabilities—an awareness that will pay off with dividends as you learn to highlight the first and deemphasize the second—know that you will always be your own worst critic. Especially as you learn to control where the attention is going, drawing it to your assets via the use of color and shape, those liabilities will recede into the background.

Spend Your Time Styling

How do you currently spend the bulk of your getting-ready time in the morning? Trying out one outfit after another in search of a magical combination that doesn't make you feel dowdy? Digging through your hamper for the one blouse that goes with your dress pants before giving up and opting for the same jeans and button-down variation you wear every day? Twenty minutes behind when your fourth rejection still has you scrambling for an alternative? These are the hallmarks of a sweaty and uncomfortable process that rarely ends in success.

Allow me to suggest a new paradigm. You calmly approach a closet that is broadly sorted by color and category—dresses, pants, shirts, skirts. Depending on your mood and what the day holds, you are drawn to one particular end of the spectrum. You ask yourself whether it's a pant, a skirt, or a dress day, and you select according to your whims, the weather, and your schedule. Once you've made your decision, you commit to it (which won't be hard once we rid your closet of those duds you have no business putting on your body) and build from there.

Ridding your closet of clothing that doesn't fit or flatter you (as we'll be doing in Chapter 5) is going to radically streamline your selection process. Instead of spending your time trying to find something decent to wear, you'll be able to spend your time deciding how to style the first item to which you gravitate. Will you dress that silk blouse down with a long, drapey sweater, or move into power-suiting territory by topping it with a structured blazer? Pop a sexy red pump with those dark gray trousers, or keep things monotone and add a punch via jewelry and makeup instead? Rough up that cocktail-party-worthy dress with a denim jacket and a pair of high-heeled booties, or take it to work with a pair of dark tights, pumps, and a blazer? It all depends on what you want your outfit to say.

Over time, you'll begin to identify the various combinations that work best, slotting them into your personal

Look Book for safekeeping (see page 238). As you play in this way, you will discover new ways to combine the pieces in your closet, or surprising ways in which a newly purchased item can transform an older outfit.

If (like many of us) you are not a morning person, consider how your grumpy starting point may be affecting your decision-making process. Given the importance of these decisions and the impact they can have on your day, you want to give yourself the greatest possible chance of success. So either try to pull out of that funk with some upbeat music, or go through the process the night before and sleep in for an extra fifteen minutes.

Make Sure It Fits

Unless you've been hiding under a rock, you are probably aware of the fact that everyone and their mother enjoy waxing poetic about French women and how *perfect* their style is and how they *never* ever get fat. But let me tell you a little something. French women—by which the world generally means Parisian women—are not necessarily all that stylish. Evidence: When they come to America, what do they buy? Uggs. I rest my case.

But here's the thing about French women: They wear clothes that fit, and they're maniacal about quality. If you've ever seen one shop, you'll know how discriminating they are about what they take home.

Though most rules are meant to be broken, if there's one that is eternal, it's the one they abide by: All of your clothing should fit as though it were tailor-made for you.

Tailor-made generally means close-fitting, and that's no accident—the more we can see of your shape, the better you will look. Why? Because if you're not dressing for your shape, your clothing will inevitably look unpolished and accidental, as if it were borrowed from someone else's closet. Worse, it will look apologetic, as though you're uncomfortable in your own skin. And most obviously, clothing that is ill-fitting simply does not flatter.

Whatever your size and shape, well-fitting clothes send the message that you're confident about your body, where ill-fitting clothes telegraph uncertainty and a lack of confidence. Clothing that is baggy—as opposed to gracefully, intentionally flowy—invites the question "What is she trying to hide?" And clothing that is too small makes you look bigger than you are, while sending the message that you may not be entirely in touch with reality.

Clothes that fit also tend to read as more stylish. Why? Because "style" is nothing more than a woman looking great in her clothes and projecting confidence. Looking not as though she is being worn by her clothes, but as though she is wearing *them*. If changing your color palette is one of the most impactful style transformations you can make, wearing clothes that fit properly is not far behind. You stand to lose anywhere from ten to twenty pounds, and to look infinitely more current and up-to-date. So without further ado, here is my five-step guide to getting the perfect fit:

1. Don't be wedded to a number. Sizing can vary wildly from brand to brand, and even within a brand, depending on the type of garment. And it can also be highly dependent on a woman's particular shape—it's not uncommon for me to see a woman who wears a four in dresses and skirts, a six in jackets and tops, and an eight in pants, or some variation thereof. So don't be wedded to a number, and don't fall into the trap of assuming your largest size is your "true" size—there is no such thing. Try on the size you think you are, try the next

size up or down if that doesn't work—and then buy for the size that flatters, not for the number.

2. Try it on. This rule may seem incredibly obvious, but I know there are women out there who hate shopping so much that they buy clothes *without trying them on*. You can probably guess how I feel about this, so I am going to *try* to restrain myself. All I will say is that fit can be difficult to predict, and that the only situation in which you can skip the try-on is when you're replacing a basic you already own. And that if you are *bananas crazy-cakes cuckoo* enough not to try on your clothes before buying them, you may need professional help of a different sort!

3. Try it on in bulk. Certain shopping situations call for a take-no-prisoners approach. If you want to find the jeans of your life, for instance, here's how to do it: Go to a department store and locate a friendly salesperson. Tell her what you're looking for and what your usual issues are. You'll soon find yourself awash in a variety of brands and fits. You may try on twenty pairs before you're done, but you *will* find the best jeans you've *ever* had.

4. Ask a salesperson for advice. "Do you think this fits me correctly, or should I try a size down?" A good salesperson will know exactly how a piece is meant to be worn. A great salesperson will be intimately acquainted with the ins and outs of sizing in that particular brand. A brilliant salesperson will be able to make accurate suggestions about what might work on your body type.

5. Get to know your tailor. Sometimes the difference between an 8 and a 10 on the scale of fabulosity is a matter of a simple tweak—and a talented tailor. Depending on the quality or desirability of the garment, springing for an alteration can be well worth the extra cost and effort. If it's not, move on. But don't assume that alterations are only for suits and other investment pieces—there's nothing wrong with altering a pair of jeans or cords if the only thing standing between you and a perfect 10 is a gap in the waist. If altering a piece is going to make you feel and look great, it's worth it.

Make Sure It Flatters

As a stylist, I consider fit a practical matter—it either does or it doesn't. But I know that for the real women I work with, fit can be highly emotional. Every day, you are buffeted with messages about what your bodies should or shouldn't look like, with pop-up ads and billboards and magazines that feature unattainable, digitally manipulated physiques that bear little resemblance to even the models who pose for them.

I know that these messages can take their toll. Your response is often to shut down, opting out of the game by telling yourself that your particular shape presents insurmountable fit challenges that just can't be overcome. "They don't make pants that fit me." "All of the clothing in the stores is made to fit teenagers." "There's only one brand that works for me—everything else is a disaster."

I've dressed women of every shape and size, and I can tell you that statements like these are simply not true. Whatever the ads may imply, these days, the real, on-the-ground fashion landscape is all about the consumer. Designers are creating jeans for every particular body type and in every possible hue; beautiful and stylish clothing that is expertly crafted to flatter plus-size women; and wardrobe solutions specifically meant to enhance women at every life stage.

There are *tons* of options out there for every body type, so it's all about seeking out those shapes that work best for you. Whether you're plus-sized, stick-straight, pear-shaped, upside-down pear-shaped (bigger on top, skinny on the bottom), apple-shaped, hourglass-shaped, petite, or extremely tall, there are great clothes out there for you. But you do need to put some effort into learning how to dress your body, as you're going to see the best results when you work with fit and proportion to flatter your particular shape.

Some universalities apply to everyone. A waist is always desirable; define your waist and you'll instantly look slimmer, sexier, and more put-together. A monochromatic outfit is slimming and elongating, as are heels, which we'll be talking about in a bit. Whatever your shape, balance is key. If you're going to do a flowy top, make sure the pants are skinny; if you're in a maxi-skirt or a palazzo pant, go for a body-skimming blouse, tank, or tee.

LONG AND LEAN. Though many women think that you super-skinny girls have it oh-so-easy, I know I don't have to tell you how untrue that can be—you are definitely not exempt from the need for a fit clinic. In clothes that are even just a little bit too big, you can easily look gaunt, as opposed to gracefully lithe, like you lost a bunch of weight and failed to update your wardrobe to suit your new shape. Skinny girls *can* work the slouchy thing, but again, you want to make sure it's in balance, and that the slouch is in the right fabric; fabric is the key difference between a piece that drapes beautifully and a piece that hangs like a very sad sack. Don't be afraid of looking too skinny in close-fitting clothes; again, that gaunt look you're wary of is the result of clothes that are too big for you. If you're small-chested and looking to add the illusion of curves on top, go for a pattern, some texture, or a ruffle.

APPLE-SHAPED AND/OR PLUS-SIZE. Women who are apple-shaped or plus-sized always, always, always want their clothing to come in at the waist. Belt it, tuck it in, or wear something structured that naturally defines or creates the illusion of a waist. My plus-size clients definitely tend to wear their clothes too big, and that's a mistake. You want clothes that *fit* the body you're in, rather than clothes that attempt to *hide* the body you're in. Hiding, as I'll say until the day I die, is never the answer. That stereotypical kaftan is *not* your friend. It's the dead opposite—as much as any of the other body types, if not more so, you want your clothes to be fitted; you'll look smaller and more feminine in structured, tailored clothing. If you want to do flowy, go for a drapey outer layer; wear it open over something more fitted to create the illusion of a smaller, nipped-in person underneath. If you're going for a print, think graphic and substantial rather than tiny and delicate—the latter can look busy on you.

PEAR-SHAPED. If you're pear-shaped, you'll always want to emphasize the smallest part of your body—drumroll, it's the waist! You'll generally want to look for clothing that is tighter on top and looser on the bottom. You will probably have an easier time with dresses and skirts than you do with pants, but take heart: A high-waisted pant with a wide leg is about to become your new best friend. The height of the waist will nip you in at your smallest point, and a bit of volume in the leg will balance out your curves. Look for a straight-leg jean as opposed to skinny, but go ahead and flaunt that bodacious rear end with a body-skimming pencil skirt when you feel like it—just make sure you wear a heel to elongate the leg.

INVERTED PEAR-SHAPED. Inverted pears (you're tiny on the bottom and bigger on top) are legally required to flaunt their legs in all fifty states. Think short skirts or a slim pant with a blouse on top. If you're larger busted, V-necks, boatnecks, and off-the-shoulder tops will help open up the neck and collarbone area and draw the eye up to your face; a crewneck can make you look a little bit confined and draw too much attention to your chest, as will patterns or textures like ruffles that add dimension on top. (If it has to be a crewneck, go for something fitted, with a scoop neckline, and pair it with a monochromatic bottom.) Seek out tailored shirts and dresses with darts or ruching to nip in the waist and minimize that unflattering shelf effect. (Side note: Ruching is every girl's best friend!)

HOURGLASS-SHAPED. Hourglass ladies need to belt it and fit it. Show those curves, and cinch in that waist. If your clothes don't come in at the waist and skim that booty, you're going to get the dreaded tent effect that camouflages your assets and turns you into a very grouchy blob. Here's what you're going to have to accept: For you, sexy works best. It's a tough row to hoe, but somebody's got to do it.

TALL GIRLS AND TINY GIRLS. Tall girls and petites can span all of the aforementioned body types, so pay attention to your individual shape. Neither of you should be afraid of popping that color or dressing to be seen, but do be aware of patterns that overwhelm you.

A special message to the tall ladies: Please, please, please stop trying to hide your height! I know where you're coming from—you feel like a giraffe in a pair of heels, and you fear drawing too much attention to yourself with any extra height. But the net result is that you wind up wearing flats when they're not appropriate for the occasion or less-than-flattering with the outfit you're wearing. *This* is what will make you look clunky and awkwardly tall as opposed to gracefully statuesque. Wearing flats with the wrong outfits just makes you look like you're apologizing for your height. Stop apologizing, and embrace the aura of influence and power that taller people naturally project. Here's the counterintuitive truth about heels: Especially for you taller, plus-size girls, a heel can actually make you look more dainty.

The Skinny Myth

Is there some part of you that believes only women who look like models can be stylish? If so, you've fallen prey to a marketing fallacy. I'm not going to lie—it can be easier to dress tall, skinny women, which is why designers use them to model their wares. Streamlined bodies don't interrupt the line of the garment, and so act as canvases that let the clothes do most of the talking. But that doesn't mean it's impossible to dress all the other kinds of bodies—and anyway, in the real world, we want you to be doing the talking.

There are plenty of stylish women who don't fit the skinny-chic mold. Think of Adele in her glamorous dresses, retro-chic hairdos, and to-die-for makeup, or the pinups of the 1950s. If you've been using your body type as an excuse for a subpar wardrobe, it's time to wake up to a new reality: Great style has very little to do with size, and everything to do with the choices you make.

Listen to What Your Clothes Are Saying

When you look at yourself in the mirror in the morning as you're getting dressed, what is the question that you are trying to answer? My guess: some variation on "Does this look okay?"

Ask the wrong questions, and you'll get the wrong answers. Yes, your outfit probably does look *okay*. But you're asking the wrong question. Instead of asking yourself, and your mirror, for confirmation that what you have on is acceptable or appropriate or even whether it's fabulous, I want you to ask yourself my golden question: "What does this *say*?"

It's a question that is infinitely powerful, nudging you into a more objective position and helping to cultivate your sense of awareness. When you ask yourself what that light blue cap-sleeved cotton dress *says*, you're moving from a superficial understanding of that garment's material qualities (lightweight blue dress to wear in warm weather) to a deeper understanding of what it *communicates*—maybe it's "sweet, unpretentious girl jonesing for some prairie time." At which point you can take a step back and evaluate whether that's the impression you wish to make at that particular moment. What do you *want* it to say? I'm sure you *are* a sweet girl, and who doesn't love a nice prairie— but is that the message you want to put out right now? Would edgy, confident, competent professional be a more productive look for you? Or accessibly sexy, flirtatious, and available full-grown woman? If it's a flattering dress and that blue is a good one on you, can you alter its message by pairing it with a navy blazer, gold chain necklaces, and a nude patent-leather heel?

Explicitly asking yourself the question of what message you are emitting puts you in the driver's seat, giving you full control over the image you create. It's powerful stuff, and the varieties and shadings are infinite. But you don't need a degree in psychology or several decades of professional styling under your belt to play this game. All you need to do is learn to ask the right question: What does this say?

Dress for the Impression You Want to Make, Not for the Occasion

Pop quiz. You've got a meeting with an important person who has the power to impact your life or career in a significant way. It could be a meeting with that prospective client whose monster account you're dying to land, a coffee with a luminary you've idolized for years and whose attention you've somehow managed to get, an interview for a dream job you can't even believe actually exists, or that end-of-year meeting with your boss in which you are finally going to make the case for that well-deserved promotion. What are you going to wear?

Before you can answer that question, you need to ask yourself this one: What is your intention for the outcome of this meeting—and what kind of an impression would be most likely to help bring this outcome about?

Think about the person you're going to meet. What is this person like? How does this person present him- or herself? If this meeting were taking place in a movie, what role would this person play—and how would you cast yours? Within the subtly shaded context of a truly conscious way of dressing, you will present yourself in a manner that is tailored to this particular situation, and to this particular person. If you can refine your understanding of the dynamics at play and go beyond the need to just look good enough, you'll have that much more power to affect the situation. You want to look put-together, sure, because looking put-together denotes success and confidence—but there's lots more at play on the subconscious level, and tapping into that is key to controlling the impression you create. Would it be in your interest to look more businesslike, or should you go casual? Should you play it soft, or go for a look that's more sleek? Conventional, or with a bit of an edge?

My work often calls for these fine-edged distinctions. Recently, for instance, my ruby-red starlet called me because she was going to be taping a companion album to the Broadway show she was starring in. The hitch? Cassie's publicist had invited a mess of journalists who'd be hanging around the studio all day. This stressed her out *immensely*. We couldn't deck her out in the full-on red-carpet treatment—she needed to look beautiful and starlike, but like a beautiful star who was hard at work taping an album.

This wasn't so much a matter of figuring out the style "etiquette" for a press conference slash Broadway soundtrack taping—there is no such thing—as it was of reading the situation and fine-tuning the messages we wanted to communicate. In the end, I put her in a navy wide-legged pant that looked luxurious but toned down and practical, a cream silk blouse whose sheen lit up her face, and an emerald-green cardigan that popped her gorgeous green eyes, loading her up with gold jewelry to tie it all together. Confident and humble, starlike and approachable, pretty and professional—she was all of these things, and she called me that night to tell me she'd gotten compliments all day.

Conscious dressing is a method with shadings far more

intricate than the usual set of rules about what to wear to a cocktail party or how to transition into spring. I don't want you following rules about what to wear to a cocktail party—instead, I want you to interrogate yourself about what it is that you want out of your experience at this cocktail party, and then dressing to suit. Is it a party where you're going to be seeing both friends and business acquaintances? Then you need to find a look that is festive yet still representative of your professional persona—and if you're on the prowl, that is also cute enough to catch the eye of that interesting fellow at the bar. If it's a party at which you are going to be introduced to your new boyfriend's parents, you'll need to consider the impression you want to make. And so on.

As with all of my beliefs about style, this method applies not only to those particularly impactful moments you know about in advance, but also to your daily life. Thinking of your outfit in terms of the various roles it communicates is actually a very fun and useful way of approaching your dress routine. I recently complimented an effortlessly stylish friend on the outfit she wore to meet me for lunch—a gray silk blouse with tiny white polka dots and a poet's collar buttoned up all the way to

Control the Juxtapositions

Here's an addendum to the rule of harmony: Juxtaposition can be a great way to make an outfit look unique, stylish, and chic—but it has to be a thoughtful juxtaposition, and not an inadvertent mishmash.

It's a method that definitely falls into the category of advanced styling, but if you're interested in experimenting with it, think of playing opposing categories off each other: tough versus feminine, edgy on top and soft on the bottom (or vice versa), soft versus coarse. A classic juxtaposition is to layer a blazer or a military jacket over a demure flower-print dress; a pair of edgy heels or boots completes the look.

Just as you can juxtapose styles and associations, you can also juxtapose fabrics: the plush coziness of a sweater coat against an ethereal wisp of a dress, the sheen of satin against the knobbiness of tweed.

It's a fun game that can result in lots of unexpected surprises. But in the end, here, too, it all comes back to harmony. These juxtapositions *must* work together to add up to a seamless, meaningful whole—which means that we're definitely getting into some challenging territory. If you're uncertain, do not proceed without the full consent and approval of Rent-a-George. (If he is not available to advise, please tweet me a selfie and I promise to get right back to you.)

her neck, high-waisted cropped gray trousers, and gray high-heeled booties. She told me she'd gone for a bit of an "old-school journalista" look that day, a response I just loved. She hadn't thrown together an outfit that seemed to match; instead, she'd had a playful role in mind, maybe inspired at first by that silk blouse, and then pulled pieces together around that idea.

Whether it's done in the spirit of play or in a take-no-prisoners, high-stakes mode, dressing this way is a powerful tool. When you consider not just how your outfit looks but what roles you are inhabiting, you are giving yourself a bird's-eye view on the overall impression you are making—an impression you can then tweak toward one role or another, depending on the circumstances.

Finish It Off with the Right Shoe

You know the old saying, "The shoe makes the (wo) man?" The truth about shoes is that they are so important, so essential to the integrity of an outfit, that they probably merit a book of their own. Even though shoes are the farthest thing from our faces, they do get noticed, and in a big way. We fetishize shoes, ogling them on passersby and even stopping strangers on the street to ask them where they got theirs. More than almost any other item a woman puts on her body, shoes function as a type of shorthand. Is she sexy, practical, busy, important? Careless, dowdy, out-of-touch? A magazine editor or a banker? They might both be wearing the same suit, but the choice of shoe (and other accessories) is often the differentiator.

We look to shoes to give us the quick-and-dirty low-down on a variety of social cues. And when the shoe doesn't fit, it's painfully obvious. How many times have you messed up a great outfit by pairing it with the wrong shoe at the last minute, and then gone on to regret your choice all evening long, feeling like an awkward teenager sidelined at the prom?

The shoes are a big deal. And if there's one thing I've learned in all my years of styling, it's that women tend to get emotional about this subject. So let me just say from the start that if back or foot problems are keeping you in flats, we're going to find a work-around. But it has to be said (and I know you saw it coming): Heels will always equal feminine, sleek, and sexy, and to my mind you can never go wrong with a leg-lengthening, height-augmenting, and drama-intensifying pair.

I'm pretty sure you know how great you look in a heel. How? Because if I ask you to dress yourself for a wedding, a black-tie event, or a job interview, nine times out of ten you are going to come back to me with a heel on. As I'll say again and again, if you want to take it up a notch, bring the items you wear for those perceived high-stakes situations into a more regular rotation. That doesn't mean I want you in a black-tie gown on your way to the supermarket. But it does mean that if you swap out your clogs for a sexy pair of heels (and add the ever-important statement necklace, bracelet, or earring), those jeans are suddenly going to be sending a very different message. Throw on an amazing heel, and an outfit that's not so exciting will *always* look like something.

With so many of the comfort brands making stylish, great-looking heels, there's no reason most of you shouldn't be able to find at least one special-occasion heel and one basic heel you can manage to wear for several hours without discomfort. Challenge yourself to look for those heels, and snag them when you find them. Stilettos aren't the only fruit—there are as many types of heel as there are washes of jean. For comfort, look for a thicker, shorter heel, or make the wedge and/or platform your friend—but just know that the higher you go, the better your legs will look.

Sometimes the issue with heels is a lack of padding in the toe box. Again, the good comfort brands will always have your back in this area, but if you fall for a shoe with a thin toe box, take it to a good cobbler and ask him to add a more cushioning sole.

The *real* challenge is finding a comfortable shoe without a heel that still looks feminine and pretty. To me, flats will always look a bit more casual and a bit less exciting—so if you need to live in them, make sure yours are as feminine and interesting and fun as possible. Pop a color, or look for great details. Ballerinas have a graceful line, so they're the best choice when you're going to be showing some leg. Moccasins, driving shoes, and classic loafers have a more substantial look that's a better fit with pants than with skirts.

I know that shoe shopping can sometimes be disappointing, traumatic even, but please don't give up on those feet. Even if you don't like ordering shoes online, you can do some great advance recon by checking out the reviews on sites like Zappos and Amazon; users on these sites tend to get very specific about the comfort issue. Once you find a few brands that work for you, check in with them every few months to see if they have anything worth trying on.

By the law of the Closet Full of Perfect 10s, (which we're going to be learning all about in the next chapter), it goes without saying that at the end of this process, every shoe in yours will be fantastic. But it's all about pairing the *right* shoe with the *right* outfit and the *right* piece of outerwear and the *right* bag (*and* the right accessories and the right makeup and the right hair). Which is why when it comes to shoes, the key words are try, try, try, and try again. Until you have every piece in your closet categorized into a mental or physical Look Book (that's coming up in Chapter 6), you're going to be doing a lot of trial and error. So get your outfit on, grab the three or more pairs of shoes you *think* might make it work, and then try each on and see which one actually looks best. The idea of trying on multiple shoes is such a simple tweak, but it's one that really works wonders.

Accessorize, Accessorize, Accessorize

I know who you are. The self-described minimalist—white T-shirt, khakis, maybe a pair of stud earrings and a watch if we're lucky—whose politicized stance against accessories is actually the result of fear and confusion. The one-bag, one-necklace wonder who refuses to switch out her accessories on the basis that she has important work to do and anyway, "real women don't switch purses." The frazzled new mom who can hardly get it together to shower. (No caricature for you, as I totally get that in a busy mom's style routine, accessories are always the first things to go.)

Mistakes one and all, as accessories are probably the most impactful way for you to alter the statement that your outfit is making. The tool to end all tools, the punctuation to any wardrobe, accessories can make a less-than-stellar outfit work for any situation or event—and they can take a decent outfit all the way to fabulous.

Women who struggle with style tend to overlook the accessories category entirely, discounting it as some kind of an optional, advanced technique they don't need to worry about. If that describes you, don't even think about skipping this section.

Many of you ignore your jewelry. But the right jewelry acts like the right colors, lighting up your face as a photographer would on a professional shoot. There's a reason most jewelry is made from shiny materials—gold, silver, diamonds and other crystals, beads, pearls. Our baubles are designed to catch and reflect light, drawing attention to the beautiful face, the slender wrist, the dainty fingers. The bling that instantly dresses up our T-shirt and jeans, accessories are what's going to make that hectic new mom's laid-back outfit look acceptable—so the extra few minutes she spends on them will be well worth her while. And if you absorb the lessons you're about to learn in the chapter on color and wear the tones and stones that complement your complexion, you'll be doing that much more for your overall palette.

Whether we're talking about jewelry, scarves, belts, or handbags, the character of our accessories also has the ability to tweak the statements our clothing is making. Just as with anything else that you put on your body, the key question—always—is, *What does this say?* What do these accessories add to the overall picture? They may be small in size, but they can transform the character of our clothing in surprising ways. Take a sweet, perhaps overly girly floral-print dress. Wrap it in a rugged woven belt, and suddenly it looks edgy. The belt adds dimension, creating a complex and interesting juxtaposition via the addition of texture and color. (It also defines the waist, always a bonus.) Throw on a pair of edgy high-heeled booties and a couple of bangles, and you've got yourself an outfit. It's all in the details, and these details can pack a punch—accessories are the theme that makes an outfit out of your separates, the statement that makes your suit stand out, the secret sauce whose spice makes an ensemble look like *you*.

Even a professional stylist won't necessarily be able to predict how something will work without seeing it on, so make sure you carefully evaluate your choice of accessories in that mirror. A gold necklace with a red dress may sound like a great idea. But if the dress is patterned and the necklace is a double-stranded tangle of gold discs, we might be getting into busy territory; conversely, if you are wearing a dress that is all one color and texture, you may want a couple of sizable or textured accessories to break things up. And of course, never forget to check the whole picture and the way your accessories are interacting with your shoes, your outerwear, and so on—your choice of shoes will most definitely affect the way a piece of jewelry looks with a particular outfit.

Getting my clients comfortable with accessorizing is both one of the most challenging and one of the most rewarding parts of my job. So many of them are afraid of it, but when they take to it—when they start to *play*—I see the lightbulb go on. At heart, accessorizing is a grown woman's version of playing with her mother's jewelry box. Accessorizing should be *fun*, and you will become successful at it when you can figure out how to take some pleasure in it. Think of it as the playful bit of dress-up you get to indulge in every morning, and you are on your way.

Consider Your Makeup

Why does a chapter titled "How to Get Dressed" include sections on hair and makeup? Because my focus in this book is not just your clothing, but the entirety of your physical self—everything that is seen and perceived by the outside world and thus contributes to those snap judgments I keep bringing up.

Hair and makeup must be considered an intrinsic part of your wardrobe transformation. Both contribute colors, textures, and messages of their own—so in the quest to create a harmonious self, you ignore them at your own peril.

Let us travel in our hypothetical time machine to your wedding day. The flowers are done, the dress is steamed, the key members of the wedding party have been located, and it's time to pull yourself together. Are you going to scrub your face, pull your hair back in a ponytail, and dust on a bit of blush? I think not. My educated guess is that after one or more consultation sessions and a trial run with a makeup artist and a hairstylist, you are going to turn up in a face full of makeup that looks fresh, natural, and beautiful—like you, only better—and a deliberately undone hairdo with a few face-framing tendrils that fall just so.

Even the most devoted non-makeup wearers and blowout haters know that when it's time to bring it, you pull out every weapon in the beauty arsenal. You wear tons of makeup to look like you're not wearing tons of makeup; to even out the skin tone, lengthen the lash, give your cheeks the glow of good health, make everything more lush. You spend hours getting that hair to look its shiniest and prettiest.

I'm not suggesting you keep full-time hair and makeup people at your beck and call (though if you have that option, I have some friends who'd love to hear from you!), but I do want you to take a good, hard look at the high-stakes/low-stakes mental divide you've erected for yourself. If you know what it takes to get your looks to a 10, why settle for anything less? Here are tools whose entire purpose is to make you look your best. Why wouldn't you want to avail yourself of them? I'm not talking about an airbrushed mask here, but about minimizing the flaws (dark circles, sallow skin) and maximizing the assets (the eyes, the bone structure, the lip). There are plenty of low-impact ways to apply the wisdom of beauty professionals to your everyday look.

If you've never had your makeup done by the pros, I highly recommend you take yourself to a department store or to your neighborhood Sephora to sign up for a makeover. For the maximum experience, you can even hire a makeup artist to come to your house; just be clear that what you're looking for is a lesson on how to do your *own* makeup. Have the makeup artist show you how to do both a day and a night look, and get some guidance on which items to purchase. Once you're on your own, keep the following tips in mind:

- Know how much is enough. Brunettes and women of color whose features are already very defined don't necessarily need to do a lot—but on the other hand, their faces can *take* a lot of makeup. For a blonde or a redhead, just a little bit of makeup can become very dramatic, which means it can be easy to overdo it—without enough makeup, however, her features can easily be lost.

■ Use makeup as a corrective. A brunette with thick eyebrows and deep-set eyes has a look that is naturally dark and intense. A smoky eye will intensify the drama (and so is perfect for evening), while a bright lipstick cheers up the whole picture. If your lashes are light, mascara should be the number-one item on your don't-leave-the-house-without-it checklist. If your skin tone veers into the yellow and green ends of the spectrum, a warming blush is on your must list.

■ Use makeup as an intensifier. Consider your assets. If your lips are beautiful, highlight them with color. If your eyes are dramatic, layer on the dark eyeliner so that they pop even more. (Eyes are tricky, so definitely consult with that makeup artist to find the techniques and shades that will work with your particular palette, eye color, and bone structure.)

- Don't ditch your makeup bag on the weekends. Particularly when you are wearing more casual outfits, makeup is absolutely key to pulling your look together. If the notion of putting anything on your face during your downtime is foreign, start with just a little eyeliner or lip gloss and see how you feel.

- Don't be afraid to go bold. One of my clients finally started rocking the fun, bright, bold lipsticks she'd been collecting for years at the office. After getting over her initial discomfort, she found herself awash in compliments like "You look like a beautiful Gypsy" and "You're so stylish all of a sudden!" (She hadn't even substantially changed her clothes yet—such is the power of a great lipstick.)

- Especially when it comes to purchasing eye shadow and lipstick, combine the makeup artist's knowledge about products and application techniques with the color know-how you're going to pick up in Chapter 4, "The Power of Color."

- Last and perhaps most important, do not forget to consider the way your makeup interacts with what you are wearing. A more subdued ensemble might benefit from a pop of color at the lip, while a bright and busy pattern could require a subtler hue. To ensure that your colors aren't clashing, you'll want to stock up on a small range of lip and eye colors so you can swap them out as needed.

Wear It with the Right Hair

Here's how *not* to get the perfect hairstyle: Pick something you like out of a magazine, take it to a stylist, and ask him or her to replicate it. The perfect haircut and color for you is not going to result from an attempt to copycat your favorite celebrity, but will instead emerge from an honest and substantive discussion with the right stylist.

The first step to getting that great cut and color is finding the right stylist and the right colorist. I can't stress this enough. If you don't already have someone who cuts and highlights your hair so well that you're constantly fielding compliments and handing out recommendations, it's time to do some research. And when I say research, I mean a serious, methodical inquiry. You should be investigating your hairstylist with the same amount of care you would put into finding the medical specialist who will save your life. Ask your friends (the ones with great hair). Ask that woman at the office, that mom on the soccer field whose highlights you're always admiring, that stranger in line at the movie theater, where they get their hair done. Because your hair is essentially a hat you are wearing every day, you really, really, really need to get it right. A few other tips to keep in mind:

- The right stylist should push you a little bit out of your comfort zone, like that personal trainer who gets the best out of you at the gym. Find someone you trust and have a discussion about what is going to work best for your hair, the shape of your face, and your lifestyle. Be honest about your reality. If you're not great at doing your own hair and can't schedule three blowouts a week, you are a prime candidate for a haircut that is wash-and-wear.

- The right colorist may not be the same person as the right stylist. Colorists are the chemists and artists of the trade. Their work can be sublime—and it can also go very, very wrong. If you are researching your stylist with the care you would expend on finding a doctor, you should be investigating your colorist with the intensity you would bring to finding a surgeon. Just as with clothing and makeup, in the realm of hair it is impossible to overstate the importance of color. Some women are blessed with the right color, the hue that enhances their complexion and draws out their eyes, and some women are not. If you fall into the latter category, consider tweaking your hair color so that it flatters you and adds a bit of drama to your overall palette.

■ Interrogate your follicles in the same way you interrogate your wardrobe. Think about what your hair is saying, and whether that message suits your age, your profession, your hopes and dreams. Curly hair can be friendly and approachable, and I'm all for curly girls embracing their natural textures—but if you're looking for sexy and polished, go for that blowout. Long hair can be beautiful, but it requires care. A bun can be the pathway to low-key elegance, or it can lead straight to the information desk at your local library.

- Don't settle for anything less than a 10. Many of us think of hair as something immutable, beyond our control. We have good hair, or we have bad hair. Not the case! You have far more control in this area than you may realize, so it's all about figuring out how to work with what you've got.

- If you have great hair, show it off! Keep it healthy and shiny and wear it down as much as you can.

- Consider the changing nature of your hair. As we get older, our hair can lose lushness and shine. The color will change. I have nothing against a beautiful silver bob, but it all depends on the gray. If yours is washing you out and making you look tired, get thee to a colorist. Rinse out the gray, and go for a tone that's a little bit lighter than your natural color; add some highlights to bring light to your face.

- If your hair is thinning or turning dry and brittle, it's probably time to go for a shorter do. Whether that's a well-manicured bob or an Audrey Hepburn crop, your hair will look fuller and healthier. I love when a woman wears her hair short and swept off her face—it can be such an elegant look. On the flip side, there's nothing wrong with faking it—consult with your stylist to find out about extensions, the secret behind many a Hollywood celebrity's lush, long mane.

- Forget the trends, and don't bother looking at what the models or celebrities are doing. Hair is far too important to be subject to the fluctuating winds of the trend machine.

- As with your makeup, consider the way your hairstyle interacts with the outfit you have on. Some ensembles require updos, and some look better with your hair flowing free. It all depends on a variety of factors, from the neckline to the style of the garment to its color and texture. (A brunette wearing a brown sweater may get lost in a sea of mud if she wears her hair down, for instance.) There's no easy way to quantify this hair-up/hair-down question into a methodology, so this is another case where you're going to have to spend the time styling it in the mirror. Try it up, and try it down—see what fits best. It should be readily apparent.

Your Getting-Dressed Checklist

Though we'll be getting into the down-and-dirty business of applying my style precepts in the coming chapters, you can start to incorporate some fundamental principles into your daily routine right away. Because it all comes down to what happens in front of that mirror, there are certain criteria you should apply to your reflection every time you are leaving your house.

1. Check the fit. Does the clothing you have on fit you correctly? If not, take it off right away and put it into a "Maybe" pile. In Chapter 5, we'll be going through your closet piece by piece, but it's never too soon to start the process.

2. Check the flatter. It's not enough for your clothing to simply fit—it must also flatter. So take a look in the mirror and make sure that at least one of your best attributes is being displayed. You don't need to show off that cleavage every day, but you want the shape of your outfit to be doing *something* for you.

3. Check the colors. Here's where we're going to take everything you're about to learn in Chapter 4 and make sure you are applying it, every day and in every way. As we get further into this process and purge your closet of the colors that don't suit you (and, eventually, stock up on those colors that highlight you at your best), this will get easier and easier. You won't be able to go wrong in this department when your wardrobe is filled with clothing in the palette you were born for—but you're still going to have to make sure that the colors you are wearing complement each other and suit both the occasion and your mood.

4. Check for harmony. Does your outfit make sense? Do the shapes, patterns, colors, styles, and fabrics all come together into a pleasing and harmonious whole?

5. Check the message. Ask yourself my golden question: *What does this say?* And what do you want to say? Does the message suit your intentions for that day, that event, that moment? Does your outfit look sad, or does it have some buoyancy? Every outfit should have a little bit of happiness, an element of interest, whether it comes from color, pattern, or shape. Is anything sticking out, in a bad way? I tend to think that women err on the side of under-accessorizing, but there is something to be said for Coco Chanel's advice to look in the mirror and take one thing off before leaving your house.

what your daily routine reveals about you

As should be obvious by now, I believe that fabulous style is a goal anyone can achieve. It is not a fixed state or an innate quality, but rather the result of a conscious and daily practice, which is why looking closely at your daily habits is key to making those big-picture changes we're after. Take a good look at the circumstances surrounding your style and you'll have a better sense of the road map for your personal transformation.

What does your dressing pattern say about you? Dig out your little black book in order to record your responses to the following prompts:

- Examine your routine. What is a typical morning like for you? Pay attention to how you feel as you're getting dressed. If the experience is chaotic, interrogate that chaos and see if you can understand where it's coming from. Can you envision a few concrete fixes that would help ameliorate your routine—getting up fifteen minutes earlier, or organizing your bag or even your outfit the night before?

■ Look into your assumptions about fit. What are some of the outfits and garments in your current wardrobe that fit you best? What is it about these pieces that works, and where do you go wrong? Do you tend to hide in tent-like clothing that throws a bolt of fabric at the perceived "problem"? Buy clothing that you know doesn't fit correctly but persist anyway, because "they just don't make clothes that fit my body"?

■ Beware of settling. I've had one client admit to frequently looking in the mirror, saying to herself, "Yup, this looks weird," and then leaving her house. It took us a while to untangle that perverse dynamic. Does it sound familiar to you? Do you sometimes (or often) leave the house in outfits you *know* aren't working? Again, look for the root cause. Are you simply lacking the basic pieces you need to make your wardrobe work? Or are you sabotaging your looks for some other, more insidious reason? Sometimes we're afraid of what might happen if we were to look our best. Is that a factor for you? Ask yourself why "weird" or "good enough" is your baseline.

- **Check your blind spots.** To which areas of your personal presentation do you turn a blind eye? Hair? Makeup? Accessories? Outerwear? Try to ask yourself the hard questions about why this is so. Did you give up on your hair somewhere along the way? Decide that makeup was too much of a chore? If your jewelry lies in a jumbled, unattended heap, it's time to untangle those necklaces and see what treasures your jewel box might hold.

■ Bring some fun into your dressing routine. What types of events do you *enjoy* dressing for? Nights out with your girlfriends? Parties and special events? Read into this comfort zone. Could you bring a bit of that spirit of play to your daily dress routine? It may be hard to imagine a rock-'n'-roll closet party taking place in the morning (sans cocktail in hand), but maybe there are little things you can do to nudge yourself into a more positive space. Turn some fun music on, or again, if you're not a morning person, consider selecting your outfits at night.

Postscript: How to Get Dressed for the Gym

It's time to talk about the gym, and I couldn't be more excited. The gym (or yoga studio or park) is the *perfect* example of an area where many of you feel like you're off the hook and anything goes. So untrue! Your future husband, your next great business connection, or your new best friend could be huffing and puffing away on the elliptical right next to yours.

Gyms are great places to meet people—one of my clients drums up the majority of her business at her tony New York gym. But even if you're not interested in this sweatier branch of networking, I'm a firm believer in the notion that any time spent out in public in clothing you don't feel great in is going to affect your overall mood. You may not be plunged into a depression by those holey oversize sweats, but you certainly aren't buoyed up and energized by them, either. And particularly when you're stepping into such a body-conscious realm, wearing clothing that telegraphs discomfort rather than confidence is sure to shape your experience.

Looking great and knowing it puts an extra pep in your step, and makes it all the more likely that you'll hit the gym in the first place. Remember, what we are talking about here is dressing for the life you want. When it comes to the gym, that means dressing for the body you want. Fresh new gym clothing, in those miraculous fabrics designed by today's savvy fitness-wear gurus to flatter and tone, can be a motivating factor in and of itself.

Because I feel very strongly about this topic, I have articulated my gym philosophy as a simple list of dos and don'ts. To wit:

1. Do not wear your boyfriend's or your husband's or your brother's or any man's clothing to the gym. This is rule number one, helpfully positioned at the top of this list.

2. Do not wear any clothing you owned in high school or college to the gym unless you are currently in high school or college.

3. Do not exercise in articles of clothing that are six sizes too big.

4. Do not exercise in articles of clothing that you usually wear to clean your house or wash your car.

5. Do not wear mismatched articles of clothing or clothing in crazy color combinations. (Graduates of Clown College should be exercising under a big-top tent.)

6. Do not wear blown-out sneakers or T-shirts with yellowed armpits.

7. *Do* wear form-fitting pants or leggings.

8. *Do* find the perfectly fitted, flattering top and buy it in a bunch of colors. (Workout tees tend not to be the most flattering, so unless you've been blessed with a natural athlete's physique, opt for the structured, slimming tops meant to work with a woman's curves.)

9. *Do* take as much pride in your gym clothing as you would in any other ensemble you would be putting together in your new, überconscious styling mode.

chapter 3

the checklist
the twenty-two items no closet should do without

*Dress shabbily and they remember the dress; dress
impeccably and they remember the woman.*
—Coco Chanel

*Anyone can get dressed up and glamorous, but it is how
people dress on their days off that is most intriguing.*
—Alexander Wang

While every closet has different needs—and you'll get a
much better sense of yours after having gone through the
closet purge in Chapter 5—there are a few unchanging
essentials I believe no closet or woman can live without.
Many of these items will sound familiar, and I'm not going
to lie to you (I would never!)—they don't vary so much,
from one book or magazine or website to the other.

There's a reason for that, and the reason is simple: They *work*. For the most part, they work because they represent the streamlined, tailored silhouettes upon which you can layer any number of pieces, in any number of styles. They work because "classic" can generally be thought of as a synonym for "simple and well made"—clothing that flatters a broad range of body types and is at home in an infinite variety of contexts.

Build on these classics, mixing and matching them with trendier and/or more inexpensive, spur-of-the-moment pieces. These are the pieces that will be the foundations of your closet. This is where you should spend your money, because these pieces are timeless—and the better their quality, the longer they will last. Because you should be able to wear them in an infinite number of ways, their cost will earn out a lot quicker than you might think.

Beyond its practicality, a closet that is well stocked with great-quality foundational garments is a closet that feels abundant, luxurious, and complete. It's a closet whose door you will be more than happy to open, knowing that it holds everything you need in order to put together outfits that will have you standing tall—no matter what the day holds.

A Closet Full of 10s

Before we get into the items on my checklist of essentials, I want to introduce you to the overarching concept you should be applying when purchasing these items—or indeed, when purchasing any item of clothing that you plan to bring into your closet. Ready?

Every single item in your closet should be a perfect 10, and nothing less.

I'll give that a moment to sink in, as I know from prior experience that you'll need to take some time with it—whenever I first tell a woman my theory of the Closet Full of Perfect 10s, she looks at me like I've just suggested she charter a bush plane and get to work colonizing some remote Alaskan outpost. I find this *so* crazy. Frankly, fashion is not all that complicated. I'm sure you manage a whole host of activities that require more of your time, energy, and intellect.

The fact that this notion seems so impossible, that even the concept of *striving for* a closet free of duds and full of impeccable clothing seems like such a stretch, is revealing in and of itself. Would you argue with the assertion that you shouldn't bring furniture into your house unless you really love it? Think of the care with which you'd shop for a new couch, or select a new set of plates. Would you argue with the idea that you should endeavor to book the very best and most memorable vacation within your budget? I'm guessing you wouldn't—so why should you treat your clothing any differently? If you want to improve the state of your wardrobe, it stands to reason that you're going to have to raise the bar on your standards for its contents.

I know what you're thinking. How the heck are you going to go from your current situation to a closet full of 10s? You're not a stylist or a millionaire. But picture this scenario: What if I told you that an impromptu camera crew had assembled at your front door, ready to film a reality show with *you* as the star? In case you're pondering flight, please accept that in this high-stakes hypothetical, there is no escape. You've got to go meet the camera crew (though there's nothing wrong with making them wait). So what are you going to put on your body? Your heart rate would skyrocket, I'm sure, but I'm confident that after an initial scramble you would open the door looking downright fabulous.

My point is, you have those 10s in your closet. You already know what they look like. And when the stakes are high, you pull them out. Whether it's for a job interview, a first date, an important meeting, or a last-minute television appearance, we all pull out the 10s when the stakes are higher.

But what does that say about how we're treating the rest of our days? Do we actually think that there is nothing at stake on those days? There *is*—we just don't see the stakes, or necessarily know about them in advance. Most of our days aren't filled with big events. So what you're doing by dressing only for the occasions you know about is closing yourself off to the opportunities you didn't know were there. And what I want you to do is *carpe diem* and seize the fashion day.

Whether we hit or miss the mark—and I'm fully aware that not everyone *will* hit it every day—the idea of the perfect 10 is a powerful goal that holds us to a higher standard than we may be used to. For many of us, a daily 7 would be an improvement. A 10? Solid gold. So the mere idea of striving for a closet full of 10s is sure to garner results.

A perfect 10 can be formal, or it can be casual—a suit can be a perfect 10, but so can a pair of jeans. Even a T-shirt or that outfit you wear to Spin class can be a 10. A 10 fits and flatters you perfectly, highlighting your best features and downplaying your problem areas. A 10 includes one or more of the colors that make you look well rested and healthy, drawing out your eyes and complementing your hair. A 10 is always in tip-top condition, with fabric that still looks fresh and new. A 10 is that item you get the most compliments on. (Pay attention to those compliments— they're one of the most direct clues as to how your clothing is being perceived, a virtual GPS that can let you know when you're headed in the right direction and when you need to readjust your course.)

Most important, a 10 just feels great. When you put it on, you feel like yourself, at your best. You feel attractive, confident, energized, and powerful. The world is your oyster, and nothing can stand in your way.

I'm confident in your innate ability to spot a 10 when you see it—and by the end of this book, your eye will be honed so you're better able to pick those 10s off a crowded rack. But first, you've got to commit to the idea of going for a 10, every day and in every way. What's holding you back?

The List

Keep the notion of the perfect 10 in mind as you begin to acquaint yourself with my ultimate list of the necessities no woman's closet should be without. Depending on the season, you may want to acquire doubles, triples, or even quadruples of some of these items, gradually layering on interest via texture, detail, and color once you've stocked up on your neutral basics.

If in the past you've avoided classic pieces for fear of their being boring—or because you naturally gravitate toward clothing that might *seem*, in the moment, like more fun—you are not alone. I've seen plenty of clients whose closets were missing these very pieces but were stocked to the brim with miniskirts, maxidresses, and unholy quantities of tank tops. But here's the thing: The items on this list are the pieces that prevent those "I have nothing to wear!" moments I'm guessing you're more than familiar with. The pieces that will prevent the haphazard, compromise-ridden work-arounds that result from a less-than-functional wardrobe. The stuff that will enable you to feel secure and confident in your ability to pull yourself together for any situation. And far from being boring, they're endlessly malleable. How you wear them is up to you.

Needless to say, every item on this list should be nothing less than a perfect 10. And that's where the real transformation comes in—via a baseline of carefully curated, perfectly fitting basics that signal your commitment to quality in everything that you put on your body. Replace your thoughtless everyday basics with spot-on, high-quality, go-everywhere neutrals and your look will be instantly transformed. Beyond that, you'll have a foundation from which to shop with confidence for a wardrobe that suits your particular needs, allowing you to assert full control over the impressions you project. On to the list:

☐ **THE CLASSIC LITTLE BLACK DRESS.** Though I do tend to try to strip the black out of the closets of the blondes and redheads with whom I work (more on that in the next chapter), I make an exception for the little black dress, also known as the LBD—such a go-everywhere icon that you simply *cannot* construct a functional closet without one. (Ask Coco Chanel, Audrey Hepburn, or Donna Karan if you don't believe me.) Having a perfect little black dress in your closet will prevent you from going into a full-scale panic every time you are invited to an impromptu event. You can dress it down with tights and boots; dress it up with heels, statement jewelry, and your most dramatic makeup; or take it to work with a blazer and a flat. Simple, slimming, lengthening, sophisticated, grown-up, tasteful, and confident, it will always be in style.

P.S. The little black dress needn't actually be so little, but it should be simple and relatively unadorned. The fit—shift, A-line, body-skimming, halter, strapless, ruched, wraparound, tailored, or floaty—is up to you. The perfect little black dress should suit both your personality and your body type.

☐ **THE SEXY, PULL-OUT-ALL-THE-STOPS DRESS.** For some of you, the LBD may fulfill this function. Regardless, all of you should be on the lookout for the magical little item I like to call "The Dress of Your Life." This isn't really a piece you can mission shop for so much as it is one that calls your name when you least expect it. Be ready to heed its call, for the power of the perfect dress is not to be underestimated. In your very best color and silhouette, this is the dress that stops a room cold and announces your arrival with very loud fanfare. Whether it's a bright red strapless number or a black-and-white polka-dotted halter or a candy-striped sundress, it's one of those statement pieces that you'll instantly recognize as being just so *you*. Don't be afraid to pull this one out regularly—and be prepared to reap the compliments.

☐ **THE PENCIL SKIRT.** Every woman needs a great pencil skirt in basic black or navy. The fit should be perfect, the fabric divine. Paired with a gorgeous silk blouse, it's a power move at the office; with a little sparkly tank and a great pair of heels, it's equally at home at a cocktail party; with a snug little cardigan, tights, and pumps, it says sexy little librarian (the kind he'd love to run into in the stacks). As you expand and diversify your wardrobe, you'll want to add on multiples of this item in your best colors—camels for a blonde, maybe a bright red for a brunette, along with tweeds, linens, silks, and patterns of all sorts. A must!

☐ **AN IMMACULATE PAIR OF BLACK DRESS PANTS.** Though lady Katharine Hepburn tended to wear hers with flats, I love a pair of dress pants and a heel, and I am always surprised by how often this item is absent from the closets of the women I work with. I know that for many of you, finding a great pair of pants can be a challenge— but without a dependable pair of polished, tailored black pants in serious fabric, your wardrobe is basically nonoperational. There are times and places and moods in which you're going to want to make a great impression, but for which skirts and dresses are not necessarily the ticket. A beautiful silk blouse, heels, and a pair of dress pants will take you anywhere, emitting a satisfying combination of confidence, sex appeal, and power.

With such an infinite variety of fits and fabrics out there in the world, there's simply no excuse for failing to nail down the ultimate pair of dress pants. Again, in this case I recommend heading to a department store, where a full spectrum of options will allow you to home in on your perfect brand. Once you find that brand, you're probably going to want to come back to it again and again—pants are not child's play. Don't be surprised or disappointed if some tailoring is called for. Nipping in the waist and taking up the length are standard practices for many of my clients. If you're well-endowed in the hip or buttock areas, you may well find that you have to size up and nip in; many are the women who wear a size eight in skirts and dresses but fit a ten in pants.

☐ **THE ULTIMATE PAIR OF JEANS.** Want to know how to get your sexy back? Find the best jeans you've ever had in your life, then put down the cold, hard cash to make them yours. That's all there is to it! In all seriousness, the level of craftsmanship that specialty designers are putting into their jeans these days rivals the exactitude of a couturier in Paris. There are jeans for every body type and for every taste, in every hue from classic denim blues to soft pastels to the brightest of jewel tones. High-waisted trouser jeans, skinny jeans, boot-cut jeans, cropped jeans, wide-legged jeans. Jeans that will define your rear end, lengthen your leg, shrink your hips, nip in your waist—the sky's the limit.

Unless you already own the perfect pair or know your brand, get thee to a department store to try on a wide variety of brands, washes, and fits. Be prepared to devote one full shopping mission to this task alone—and do not surrender until you've found the jeans that make you gasp with glee, the fit-you-like-a-glove pair that makes you want to run home and try on every top and flirty pair of heels in your closet. If you don't have a pair of jeans you feel 100 percent confident about, your world is about to be turned around. And if you're lucky enough to find this fit in a lower price bracket (some women aren't), go to town.

☐ **THE SILK BLOUSE.** Whether it's a button-down affair or a flowy boatneck tunic, a white or cream silk blouse in your best silhouette is going to act as the cornerstone of a new army of amped-up basics in your closet. More than just another item on your checklist, it stands for a commitment to improving the general level of quality in your tops, an area that is often sorely lacking in women's closets.

I get what's going on here. You sweat (who doesn't?), and sometimes you spill, and because your tops tend not to last as long as the other items in your wardrobe, you're loath to spend money on them. But the net result is that you're left with loads of subpar, low-quality goods in the area of clothing you wear closest to your face—that is, the area that is 100 percent most impactful in drawing attention (or not!) to your face and in giving you the presence you deserve. So start with one beautiful, quality blouse to tuck into that pencil skirt, wear under that blazer, or throw on over your jeans (a look I *love*), and see where it takes you. Odds are that after you've experienced the power of a really great top, you'll be raring to acquire more. In any case, great tops needn't be expensive—they just need to be thoughtful.

☐ **THREE PERFECT TEES.** Similar to the silk blouse, but with a more casual aim, updating the T-shirts in your wardrobe is one of the most efficient ways of achieving an upgrade that is immediately impactful—in fact, this may be one of your most critical moves, as our casual clothing is where we tend to commit the most egregious of our fashion sins. In considering your upgrade, I strongly urge you to stretch your conception of the fair price of a tee. The best-looking tees, the ones you admire on other women, *do* cost more money; they're the tees in luxurious fabrics by James Perse and Splendid, the tees that automatically upgrade your outfits while shedding many pounds from your frame. Down a notch will be the great basic tees from places like American Apparel, Banana Republic, and J.Crew. Buy them in a range of silhouettes—crewneck, boatneck, V-neck, or scoop—stocking up on neutrals and the pop colors you're going to be learning all about in the following chapter.

☐ **THE CASHMERE SWEATER.** What can you do to look put-together in a simple pullover and slacks or jeans? Make that pullover a gorgeous cashmere sweater in one of your best colors. If the fabric specification strikes you as overly precise, I'm guessing you don't have much cashmere in your wardrobe. Like the silk blouse and the upgraded tee, the cashmere sweater is a case where the material adds up to an item that transcends its inferior equivalents. Whether it's a V-neck, a crewneck, a boatneck, or a scoop, a cashmere sweater's luxurious weave will be appreciated not just by the lucky wearer for its unbeatable softness, but by even the most casual of observers for its readily apparent polish.

Delicate, expensive-looking, and flatteringly

unbulky, the goat's wool is widely considered the finest of the bunch. It's a magical fabric that actually becomes softer with age, is intensely vibrant, feels amazing, doesn't tend to pill or wrinkle, maintains its shape over time, is both warmer *and* far lighter than regular sheep's wool, and, in lightweight weaves, is breathable enough that it can be worn through the spring. A properly cared for cashmere sweater can last a lifetime—so it's a perfect example of an item where the initial investment will more than earn itself out over the years. Though cashmere is available in a range of price points and doesn't need to cost a bundle, to me it will always be a signifier of abundance: a luxurious, self-affirming message that boomerangs its way out into the universe and comes back around to you.

☐ **TWO PERFECT CARDIGANS.** Many of you use your cardigans as safety blankets, hiding less-than-toned upper arms or midsection woes in worn-out, stretched-out iterations of what *should* be a great-looking, go-anywhere kind of piece. What we're talking about here is an upgrade. Your sweater collection should include one fitted, classic, slim, and versatile layering piece you can wear over dress pants or with that pencil skirt; as well as one drapier, longer, and more deconstructed cardie to throw over jeans and a great tank on nights and weekends. Belt those cardigans, work those cardigans, own those cardigans. Though I love a boyfriend blazer over a flirty, romantic dress, a beautiful cardigan can look just as great.

☐ **A FITTED BLAZER.** If you're strictly a cardigan or a denim jacket girl, don't even think about passing the fitted blazer by. This one is very high up there on the ladder of style transformations, an instant shot of presence and tailoring that pulls you together to dramatic result. What else turns jeans and a T-shirt from a weekend standard into a meeting-ready power statement? Whether it's part of a suit (which I recommend, as it multiplies your options) or a perfectly fitting separate, a great blazer will define your shoulder (making you look simultaneously slimmer and more powerful); radically nip in your waist (always desirable); create interest around your face, drawing the attention right where you want it (a lapel is a beautiful thing); and keep you cozy in the chilliest of offices and restaurants.

The color is up to you, but make sure the fit suits you—cropped or long, edgy or more classic—and makes sense for your closet. A black or navy version is going to give you the most bang for your buck, but if you already have one of those, you can't go wrong with a blazer in one of your great pop colors. Once you've made your purchase, I highly recommend that you wear the *heck* out of this item. Come fall, throw it on over those wafty summer dresses with tights and a pair of boots.

☐ **A CLASSIC FITTED TRENCH.** Those of you in rainy climes will want to make sure to add this springtime necessity to the list. Down with fly-fishermen's parkas masquerading as streetwear! I don't want to see you in a zip-up polyester-nylon blend unless I'm running into you at the top of a mountain. A lightweight, versatile trench should take care of all your windy, rainy-day needs in style, looking just as great over a pair of jeans as it does over a shift dress. While I love a trench in a classic color like khaki or navy, a cherry red or kelly green can brighten up the cloudiest of days. It's one of those pieces that are so simple, yet so graceful and timeless and cinematic—I just love the quiet drama of a gorgeous trench.

☐ **A GREAT WINTER COAT.** If you live in a cold climate and are in want of a great-looking winter coat, add this solid investment piece to your list. There may be a time and place for a puffy down coat, but if it's your only winter-wear option, you're doing yourself a serious disservice. Shabby outerwear is a surprisingly common occurrence among even otherwise well-dressed women, and this is one I just don't get. Why drop all that money on a fabulous designer dress and gorgeous shoe, spend all that time blowing out your hair and applying your fiercest makeup, only to top it all off with the equivalent of your grandmother's bathrobe?

Since your outerwear makes your first impression, it should be a downright showstopper that's nothing less than immaculate. And because classic is the fastest shortcut to immaculate, I recommend going with a versatile double-breasted silhouette with a face-framing collar such as a car coat or with a longer, single-breasted coat. Especially if it's a long coat, keep it fitted so that we can see the outline of your body. All that time in Pilates class goes to waste if your coat is adding on an extra ten pounds!

□ **ONE BLACK PUMP, ONE NUDE HEEL.** If you've gotten this far in life without a sharp, comfortable, versatile, and sexy black pump, I shudder to think of what you've been wearing on your feet. The black pump or slingback heel is just as essential as the jeans you live in, the little black dress that saves the day, the gorgeous, color-saturated scarf that brightens up your face. Without them, you're sure to be concocting weird work-arounds and compromises that have you dressed in one of those almost-there outfits.

In so many cases, a chic black pump is the finishing touch that will effortlessly and harmoniously complete and upgrade your look, lengthening the leg and adding that ever-so-welcome dash of height, presence, and femininity. *Please* don't let me see you pairing that pencil skirt with anything else. Same goes for the nude heel, which has the added benefit of seamlessly blending with your skin tone to create the absolute longest line possible. If a nude heel is a new addition to your closet, be prepared to become absolutely addicted.

While I love a statement heel in a pop color, rare is the outfit that I don't recommend pairing with the subtly sexy, always fashionable nude heel.

☐ **THE BALLERINA FLAT.** If you've been plodding around in a hideous pair of orthopedic-grade clunkers, start your shoe makeover with a graceful pair of ballerina flats in black, nude, silver, or gold and go from there. I'm pretty sure that once you make the switch, you'll be itching to beef up your collection of pretty and functional flats, be they sandals, loafers, driving shoes, moccasins, or oxfords. Don't be afraid of experimenting with color or pattern in the shoe area. Just as you're going to do with your closet, you'll want to take inventory of where you stand and take appropriate action. While brown can be useful, if your shoe rack is a sea of mud you're limiting yourself to an unchanging earth tone statement—and there's so much more to life than that! Think of these comfort creatures as jewelry— they should be just as fun, playful, interesting, and noticeable.

☐ **THE CITY SLICKER SNEAKER.** In the name of all that is sacred and holy, please stop wearing your worst pair of beat-up gym sneakers as regular weekend footwear. If you're a sneaker girl, it's time to go out and find yourself an adorable, colorful, and stylish nonathletic pair to kick around in. Here's one area where I don't mind you following the trends—sneakers are always changing, so check out the scene and find a pair that works for you. With so many affordable options available, there's no excuse for looking like Melanie Griffith in *Working Girl* in this day and age. Just like the T-shirt upgrade, this swap is one that will instantly do wonders for your casual palette, turning your messy jeans routine into a cute and chic, Sunday-at-the-museum-worthy ensemble. Retire those bedraggled kicks by donating them to a sneaker-recycling charity, or save them for moving day.

☐ **THE GIANT BLACK WRAP.** Could there be a more perfect example of dressing for unforeseen eventualities than the impossibly soft, exaggeratedly proportioned black wrap? Here is an item that guarantees you'll never be caught in a chill without a solution that is at once glamorous and ever-so-cozy. Having a giant wrap in your closet means you don't have to worry about investing in expensive outerwear for a one-off black-tie event—

just throw it over your little black dress (or whatever fabulous ensemble you happen to be wearing) and you're good to go. At the office, it's the perfect insurance against those chilly AC drafts. And on a subzero plane trip, it morphs into a luxurious blanket. Instant glamour and drama. (Go for the cashmere here if you can.)

☐ **A VARIETY OF COLORFUL SCARVES.** How do I love a voluminous, colorful scarf? Let me count the ways. One of my absolute favorite accessories, and one of the easiest to pull off, the scarf is an oft-underappreciated item. First and foremost, I love the scarf for its power to illuminate a woman's features—as a great swath of one of your very best colors, placed right beside your face. (We're not talking about your mother's dainty, printed silk scarf here, though that item does have its place . . .) I love it for its ability to create movement, to add interest to an otherwise plain outfit. And I love it for its well-known capacities as a temperature regulator, keeping us comfortable in that unexpected spring breeze or in those freezing winter gusts. For its economical nature and its supreme adaptability, I hereby nominate the scarf as my number-one must-have accessory. It's also one of the easiest and cheapest spur-of-the-moment purchases you can make.

☐ **THE STATEMENT EARRING, BRACELET, AND NECKLACE.** As you'll hear me say throughout this book, statement jewelry is the secret sauce that can make something powerful, gorgeous, and memorable out of the simplest of outfits—from a plain, monochrome dress to your favorite jeans and tees. In this instance, what do I mean by statement? A piece that shows up and really registers, as opposed to those delicate necklaces and bracelets we might cherish for their sentimental value. Think cuffs or oodles of bangles; sizable, colorful beaded necklaces; multiple ropes of pearls instead of that single delicate strand; playful oversize cocktail rings. Don't make the mistake of saving it up for special occasions; statement jewelry can be *the* key to turning a weekend outfit from drab to fab. The best part? Statement jewelry is fun to collect and can be cheap as all get out.

☐ **A SMALL TO MEDIUM GOLD OR SILVER HOOP.** Not every outfit cries out for a statement earring—some ensembles call for nothing more than a simple glint of light-catching metal about the face. For that, a basic gold or silver hoop is the perfect solution. More visible than a stud, yet still just as neutral in terms of their style statement, hoop earrings are the little black dress of jewelry. Sometimes, however, even a simple hoop may be too much; when you're doing a very dressy look and going dramatic with the hair and makeup, you may want to play the jewelry way down, adorning your outfit with nothing more than a subtle, delicate bracelet.

☐ **A NEUTRAL HANDBAG.** Some women *love* their purses; others just cannot be bothered, and are happy enough to stash their belongings in dingy beat-up totes. It's just a bag to put stuff in, right? Wrong. If you don't have a real, grown-up handbag in a size that's practical for you and in a neutral black, gray, brown, or tan, add this item to your list. While you may think of your bag as an item you are *carrying*, and therefore less deserving of attention than an item you are *wearing*, anything you hold on your body becomes part of the overall impression you are creating. A mismatched or slovenly bag has the same effect as an ill-suited piece of outerwear, ruining the picture you've gone to so much trouble to paint. So choose wisely when it comes to your handbags, especially if you are a person who tends to use the same bag day after day; a neutral will stand the best chance at seamlessly blending in with your overarching palette.

As for the question of whether a bag needs to be costly, it's a biggie. In an ideal world, you will invest in quality handbags that will stand the test of time; but purses can be very expensive, and I know that not every woman is the designer bag type. If you're not looking to invest, keep the silhouette clean and the bag will look more expensive. I love the classics: the Kelly bag, the sack, the bucket bag, the bowling bag, and the evening clutch—also great for daytime use.

☐ **A GREAT PAIR OF SUNGLASSES.** Like an atrocious piece of outerwear, a bad pair of sunglasses can completely wreak havoc on an otherwise lovely style statement— and sadly this is a not-uncommon gaffe. Do *not* settle for that pair of fluorescent wraparounds you picked up at the local pharmacy when you lost your good shades on your last vacation! As with anything we put on our bodies, any element that is incongruous with the rest of our look is going to pull the attention away and create confusion. It's such a small detail, but such an important one—because you wear them on your face.

Great-looking sunglasses don't have to be expensive, though in my opinion, anything you're going to be wearing on or near your face is ripe for scrutiny and is thus a good candidate for investment. Whatever the price point, do try on a bunch to make sure that you wind up with a pair that suits your bone structure.

☐ **THREE TO FOUR QUALITY BRAS.** If you've never had yourself professionally fitted for a bra, get thee to a bra whisperer as soon as humanly possible; every town has at least one. Most women wear the wrong bra size, a tragedy that causes any number of ills from drooping breasts and pinchy straps to the dreaded back fat. Finding your true size can be revolutionary. The right bra, in the right size, can instantly make you lose ten pounds, radically transforming your silhouette and the way your clothes hang on your body.

If there's a shirt or dress in your closet that you haven't been wearing because you've been lacking the right undergarment, bring it with you to your fitting—your bra whisperer should be able to help you find the right bra or camisole for that particular style. While you're at it, take care of any other lingerie needs. Would that body-skimming wrap dress benefit from a little Spanx action? Is your panty drawer in disarray? Remember, great style starts from the inside out—which is why neglecting those inner layers is a terrible idea.

Mix and Match

The twenty-two pieces of clothing on this checklist are endlessly useful, providing a solid baseline on which to build a wardrobe that expresses your unique sense of style. To prove it, I've assembled some of my favorite ways to mix, match, and style these pieces for maximum versatility. For more ideas on how to style your basics, check out my Pinterest boards—I'm constantly updating them with examples of the beautiful, wearable looks I find online.

Six Better Ways to Wear a Jean

Just like dark and neutral colors, jeans can become a fall-back "basic" we wear with an utter lack of consciousness. We consider them a neutral, and we put little thought into when and how we wear them. That's a starting point that never ends well. But with a little bit of imagination, a jean can add up to big drama. In praise of the all-American wonder, here are six ways to spruce yours up (though I could go on and on and on):

1. Wear them with an expensive or expensive-looking suit jacket like a shrunken bouclé number (very Chanel) or a navy blazer, plus a slim-fitting tank or tee and lots of chains and pearls.

2. Pair them with a feminine silk blouse, big statement earrings, and a heel.

3. Top them with a gorgeous cashmere sweater and a statement necklace.

4. Flirt them up with eveningwear—a sequined or silk halter top, dangly earrings, and a heel.

5. Go glam with a tuxedo jacket, a silk tank, and a statement heel. (This look works best with black or dark denim.)

6. For summer and spring, wear them with a boldly patterned statement top and a wispy, barely there pair of sandals.

Six Ways Not to Look Boring at Work

Even women with the best of style intentions can fall into a rut when it comes to dressing for the workplace, and it's no surprise: Striking the balance between self-expression and a look that's work-appropriate can be a challenge for even the most naturally style-inclined.

But the great thing about a closet that's outfitted with a core of classics is that it's very hard to go wrong. It's all about layering interesting accessories, footwear, and tops with those trusty standards—a foundation of beautiful work-appropriate basics gives you the security to be able to experiment without fear.

The importance of looking great at work cannot be overstated. In fact, it's usually one of the first areas in which people look to up their game. And for good reason: Your self-presentation in the workplace can have serious ramifications on your influence, your salary, and ultimately on your success. (If you don't believe me, ask the coterie of experts who help those politicians select the color of their ties.)

The impact of your work will have a far greater reach if people can actually see you, so it's never in your interest to adopt an office uniform that recedes into the background. One of the best things you can do for yourself is to dress to be noticed. Here's how:

1. The easiest way to add interest to your work ensembles is by popping a color. Don't be afraid to wear those bright colors to the workplace—color can command attention and convey power, so it most certainly *isn't* out of place at the office.

2. Keep an eye out for feminine, interesting suits. A suit doesn't have to be boring—think pencil skirt with a kick pleat, or jacket with an open, ruffled neckline. It's all about the details.

3. Make a suit your own by pairing it with colorful

and/or patterned underpinnings and statement jewelry. To soften a structured suit, incorporate delicate, feminine fabrics like silk, lace, or translucent chiffon in your blouses and tanks.

4. Work the (office-appropriate) sex appeal with your footwear. An edgy heel can take an outfit from staid to powerful and feminine in a flat second.

5. Accessorize, accessorize, accessorize! When it comes to work basics that won't put your colleagues to sleep, it's all about adding your own flair and personal touch via statement-making jewelry and footwear that doesn't have to cost a bundle.

6. Do not fear the colorful daytime lip! While sultry dark eyes definitely have a nighttime vibe, a colorful lip works very well by day and can be a great way to add a little extra oomph to a neutral, dark, or quiet outfit.

Six Ways to Go from Day to Night

If your response to the words "day to night" is an involuntary eye roll, I don't blame you. This overused expression leaves many of us wondering whether anyone actually does change their outfit when the sun goes down. Here's why you should refocus your gaze: You owe it to yourself to be fully present to your postwork plans, whether we're talking cocktail party or dinner with the girls. Transitioning to an outfit that's carefully clued in to its context means you are giving those postsundown hours their due. (They're just as important as the daytime hours, if not more!) It also eliminates statement confusion—you won't go to work looking like you're at an event, or to an event looking like you just came from work. And as I've said, when we dress only for the opportunities we know about, we're closing ourselves off to the opportunities we couldn't have predicted. In that spirit, here are six easy, handbag-friendly ways to take your outfit from day to night:

1. Add drama to your makeup via a smoky eye, a dark lip, a false lash.

2. Add edge and theater with a piece (or two) of bold statement jewelry.

3. Switch out your practical flats for a pair of edgy heels—think strappy, metallic, studded, or vivid.

4. Transfer the essentials from your day bag into a sequined clutch.

5. Pull your hair into a high, slicked-back ponytail or a low, messy bun.

6. Do a reveal: Wear a silky backless top or a sexy dress under a blazer or cardigan during the day. After nightfall, remove the outerwear.

Five Ways to Improve Upon a Legging

I don't subscribe to the school of thought that says leggings only belong on model-type bodies. My issue with leggings isn't so much with the women who wear them as it is with the way in which they are typically worn— as throwaway, throw-in-the-towel garments akin to your worst pair of sweats. And if that's how you've been wearing yours, honey, I'd probably *rather* see you in sweats. In the name of all that is decent, here are five ways to improve upon a pair of leggings. (*Do* make sure that yours are fully opaque, and that you're wearing them with tops that fall to the hip or below.)

1. Cozy up for travel by wearing them casually, with an oversize cashmere sweater and a cute flat.

2. Dress them up with a tunic-length silk top and an edgy pair of short boots with a bit of a heel.

3. Wear them for night with a longer fitted blazer or tuxedo jacket with a sexy underpinning, a statement earring, and a strappy heel.

4. Fearlessly go to and from the gym or your yoga class by topping them with a casual oversize jacket and a cotton tunic.

5. For a day look, try them with a cashmere sweater tunic with a flat high boot, some bangles, and a long, beaded necklace.

Five Ways to Give Yourself a Waist

Although we've already spent some time on the importance and benefits of defining the waist, particularly for the curvier girls, allow me to reiterate: Muumuus have no place in the George B Style universe! Show your waist and you will *always* look thinner. How to go about that?

Some clothes are intrinsically structured, naturally doing the nipping in for you. But a flowier ensemble may benefit from a little extra help in this area.

1. Belt it! When in doubt, go for the belt. Gather your clothes in from the outside, with a wide statement belt worn over your dresses, blousier shirts, or cardigans. Though many women fear the belt because they don't know what to do with it or fear it will look busy, it can be one of the fastest ways to transform an outfit that isn't quite coming together. A big, thick belt can have a corseting effect, and a slimmer belt can similarly nip in the waist while acting as a delicate piece of jewelry.

2. One of the easiest ways to give yourself a waist is by tucking in your shirts. Particularly with items like A-line skirts, whose line naturally comes in at the waist and wings out, a tucked-in shirt gathers in your line for a look that is polished and svelte, where a flowy shirt would create an unflattering head-to-toe triangle effect. Tucked-in shirts also tend to add up to a look that's more put-together.

3. Look for clothes with a waistband, ruching, or darting, and for body-skimming tops and dresses with a bit of stretch. These are the clothes that will naturally define your waist—no extra work needed.

4. Slim your natural waist by giving yourself the gift of Spanx. Many of my actor clients swear by it and would not be caught dead on the red carpet without the best little body-smoothing secret in show biz.

5. To shrink a waist, top a flatteringly dark, body-skimming tank top with a lighter-colored or bright blazer or cardigan; or wear a bright underpinning and belt the outside of a dark jacket or cardigan.

How to Wear It on the Weekend

Anyone can throw on a party dress and a pair of heels and look great—but in my opinion, the real test of a woman's style is how she looks when she's off the clock, in jeans and a T-shirt. In fact, how to dress on the weekend is one of the biggest questions I get from clients. It's somewhat of a myth that a casual look is easier to pull off than a formal or professional ensemble. If you need to pull it together for a fancy event, you go out and buy that beautiful dress. Easy enough. But how do you work it in a pair of jeans? It all goes back to the same principles I've been hammering home throughout this book. Knowing your colors (you'll get acquainted with them in the next chapter). Knowing what cuts flatter your shape. Paying attention to the way the whole picture comes together.

Though I'm using the word *weekend*, I get that today's technology and changing work culture have turned that into a somewhat fuzzy concept. Whether we're tapping out emails on our phones, juggling freelance gigs on the ever-glamorous "flexible" schedule, or working the full-time, unpaid gig that never sleeps—hello, motherhood!—for many of us, the weekend is no longer a strictly delineated period of time. If that describes your schedule, go ahead and take a more expansive view on the word: the "weekend" can be any time you *feel* that you don't need to worry about self-presentation or can take it down a notch. And that, as you can probably guess, is an assumption with which I fundamentally disagree. I am a *giant* advocate of looking flat-out fabulous on the weekend (whatever that term may mean to you).

Granted, fabulosity itself means different things to different people, but I think we can all agree that it generally does not involve a pair of sparkly purple clogs—nor does it call to mind your husband's windbreaker, a faded long-sleeved tee that predates the invention of stretch fabric, or the old maternity jeans you hung on to because it just doesn't get any better than pants with an elastic waist. (Oh yes, I know *all* about this shameful little secret.)

The Principles of Weekend Style

The rules of perception and projection do not take catnaps on the weekend. Our clothing still does the talking for us, long before we have a chance to open our mouths. People still take notice and make snap judgments, and our sense of self is just as heavily implicated as it is during the week.

Before you accuse me of trying to take away your few precious moments of self-accepting schlubbyness, let me assure you that there is nothing uncomfortable about the weekend clothing toward which I steer my clients, or about the clothing I wear when I'm running around town. Comfortable or casual does not have to mean unattractive or messy—there's no reason it can't be just as graceful and inviting as your more "put-together" looks. But because so many of us are conceptually flummoxed by the notion of pulling ourselves together to relax, I've gathered a list of organizing principles for great weekend style.

DON'T BE AFRAID OF BUYING WEEKEND CLOTHING. Many of us feel guilty spending any money at all on weekend apparel, as if our stuff isn't earning out its price tag unless we're actually wearing it while we're on the clock. Could this outlook *be* any more problematic? I'm assuming you don't have similar issues spending money on quality food, entertainment, day trips, and other forms of weekend "luxuries."

Why apply a different standard to the stuff touching your naked skin?

DON'T SAVE UP THE GOOD STUFF FOR SPECIAL OCCASIONS. Life is not a series of special occasions. Life is the routine we live day in, day out. So don't save up your "good" jeans for nights out. Wear that sexy pair of jeans on the weekend with that gorgeous cashmere sweater and that fantastic fitted outerwear piece. Take the stuff that makes you feel terrific out of its special-occasion ghetto and bring it out into the world where the rest of us live. If those pieces feel overly formal to you, there are plenty of ways to dress them down, some in this chapter, and more throughout this book.

TAKE YOUR WORK CLOTHES OUT TO BRUNCH. Contrary to popular belief, anything you wear or used to wear to work can and should be dressed down for the weekend or the playground. I want you to get the most wear possible out of the quality pieces in your closet—*that's* how you get a return on your investment, and it's also how you get the best looks. Remember the high/low or ladylike/rugged concept of juxtaposition: Pair that blazer with a jean, and wear those tailored pants with an oxford or a drapey sweater.

MAKE STATEMENT JEWELRY AND BIG, BEAUTIFUL SCARVES YOUR NEW BEST FRIENDS. There's a reason scarves feature so prominently on my checklist. The plainest outfit in the world—jeans and a white tee—can become dramatic and lovely with the addition of a floaty scarf in a color that illuminates your face. Same goes for pairing casual clothes with statement jewelry—*that's* how you keep casual from looking schlumpy. Do not neglect your accessories on the weekend; if anything, that's when they're going to have to work even harder.

INVEST IN CASUAL OUTERWEAR AND SHOES. The perfect fitted jean jacket or a trench that goes from the office to the playground—that's the difference between a put-together weekend look and walk of shame in your husband's Budweiser windbreaker. Nobody's going to notice those sexy jeans if you cover them with a pile of rags! Same goes for the footwear: You'll need a variety of beautiful and comfy flats and walking shoes to take you everywhere you need to go. Ballerina flats, loafers, driving shoes, flat boots, wedges, cute sneakers (yes, even the sneakers must be cute!), and so on.

chapter 4

the power of color
identifying the colors that work for you

The best color in the whole world is the one that looks good on you.
—*Coco Chanel*

If you're like most of my clients, you are about to experience a transformation of seismic proportions. And you're going to get there by making the simplest tweak of all: adjusting the reigning palette of your wardrobe.

The concept of knowing your colors, those hues that suit your skin tone, eye color, and hair color, is one that has fallen by the wayside in recent years, carrying as it does a whiff of the Tupperware party and the mail-order catalog. Dust off those paint-by-the-numbers associations, because we're going to be bringing the color chart back, in a *major* way. I am not exaggerating when I say that 70 percent of what you're doing wrong can be addressed with a tweak to the colors you live in.

Why? It all goes back to the idea of harmony. The clothing you put on your body should never be considered separately from the totality of the picture that you are creating—a painting that cannot help but involve the color of your hair, your eyes, your skin. Think about it: Would you throw on a bright yellow hat without thinking about whether it clashed with the rest of your outfit? Well, that hat is your hair—and it's a hat you wear every day. The same goes for the rest of the colors with which you are naturally endowed.

To ignore your natural base palette is to consign yourself to a lifetime of clashing, of wearing ensembles that not only wash out your skin tone but also just don't look quite right. We want to do more than just avoid clashing, so in this chapter we're going to learn all about which colors play up your natural palette, bestowing upon you the glow of good health (and hours of blissful sleep) and punching up the light in your beautiful eyes.

Never underestimate the power of color, not only as it relates to your coloring, but also as a tool that can transform your mood and the impression you project.

My Color Philosophy

I *love* color. When I wake up feeling down, I take the opposite approach from most people. Instead of giving in to my mood and hiding out in drab or dark colors, I reach for the brightest, happiest hues in my closet. The result? An instant mood boost that tastes a whole lot better than a shot of wheatgrass!

I love color in my own wardrobe for its power to totally turn my outlook around, and for the cheer it spreads to those around me as well. I love color because I love being noticed (this may not come as a shock!), and I love its ability to make big, bold statements that speak volumes.

In the arsenal of style, color is a powerful tool, a complete vocabulary that is too often overlooked. Done right, it can spread positivity, calm, exuberance, competence, playfulness, drama (the good kind), or sensuality wherever it is perceived. If I'm starting to sound like I'm part of a cult, so be it. I am a color fanatic, and I'm not afraid to say it!

Color is *huge*. It changes everything. We pay interior designers to make sure our rooms elevate our moods—so why wouldn't we grant the same degree of attention to its role in our clothing, this second skin we carry around with us all day?

Mood manipulation aside, my color philosophy boils down to a simple formula that mirrors my overall approach to clothing: I want you to be *seen*. And when you are wearing the right colors, we see *you*, not the clothing, though we don't necessarily know why.

Counterintuitively, being seen is not necessarily always the result of wearing the brightest colors (though I do love to play with them). I often see clients trapped in the habit of wearing only dark and muted hues. Worn without intention, these can translate to an overarching look that lies at the junction of Drab City and Depressing Town. Sometimes getting them comfortable with the lighter end of the palette—creams, grays, whites, and camels—is the move that allows their features to shine through, that makes them more visible. Color is funny like that.

In general, I always want to get my clients comfortable in a wider range of hues, a range that gives them more latitude in terms of the messages they are putting out. Every woman, whether she's a dark brunette or a pale redhead, should have at her disposal a range of flattering colors that encompass light neutrals, soft and cheerful hues, and super-vibrant "pop" colors that make a big bold statement. It's all a matter of finding the particular hues that work for you.

In this chapter, and in the color primer in the color insert, you'll learn to identify the hues that make you sing. You may be surprised at what you find out. I'm always stunned by how frequently I see clients who are totally convinced that they already know their best colors—and by how frequently they wind up being *dead* wrong. Blondes with a closetful of brunette clothes, I'm coming after you!

You always want a color to be doing *something* for you. Does it bring out the color of your hair? Make you look tan? Make your pallor look lush and delicate rather than sickly? Pop your eyes (one of my favorite things to do)? One of the biggest shifts you can make is to interrogate the colors you have on and make sure they are actively working *for you*, and not against you.

Your True Colors

How do I determine which colors are right for my clients? I begin with the color of their hair—because it's generally the most saturated hue on a person's body, it makes for an obvious starting point. It's a clearer benchmark than skin tone, which encompasses a million and a half shades between here and eternity and changes depending on season. But skin tone *is* crucial, and you'll never know whether a particular color works for you until you see it next to your face. So in this chapter and in the color primer in the color insert, I'm going to be breaking down your colors according to your hair and assigning you a color category you'll use to identify your palette; but whether you're a Honey, a Caviar, a Copper, or a Silver, you'll want to play around within your category to see what works for your particular skin tone.

If you dye your strands, should you map your colors according to your natural-born hair color or your chosen hue? It's a complicated question. Because your hair presents such a wide swath of color so close to your face, its shade is important, regardless of whether it is natural or not. But if your platinum blond hair is joined by the olive skin of a dark-eyed brunette, your best bet will be a sampling across both of these categories. So check them both out below and in the color insert, and see what works.

After hair color, the natural hue to which I want you to pay the most attention is the color of your eyes. We always want to draw the focus to the eyes, the window to the soul, and the secondary pop of color that animates our base palette. The eyes speak volumes, and the more we can draw them out, the louder their statement will be.

If you're feeling overwhelmed, know that in this area a little bit of focus goes a long way. Just by bringing your attention to your colors, by posing the question of whether a particular color is right for you, you are embarking on a process that is going to be nothing short of transformative. As you start developing your consciousness, you'll soon find yourself able to pull a shirt up by your face and make a quick-fire determination about whether it's doing anything for you.

When a color is the right one for you, you'll know right away. The best colors make us look healthier, more vital, more alive; they may also make our eyes look more vivid. The worst colors immediately wash us out, making us look pale and tired. Here's a rule of thumb: If a shirt fits but is somehow making you feel less than attractive, the issue is probably the color.

Read on to find out what your hair color means for your palette, but know that color is endlessly complex and individual. What looks fantastic on one brunette may not work for another—and what looks great on you at the height of summer may not work in the depths of winter. Color is changeable, and skin tones are variable. These categories are elastic, so use them as the guidelines that will help you develop your own instincts about what works best for you. When in doubt, check in with your good friend Rent-a-George—it always helps to have a second opinion.

Honey (Warm Sunny Blondes)

Though we've all drunk the Kool-Aid on how black is the perfect, oh-so-basic color for everyone, when it comes to blondes and redheads, I couldn't disagree more. And that's why one of the very first things I do when I come into a blonde's orbit is have a little talk with her about the black in her closet. Don't get me wrong—black doesn't necessarily look bad on a blonde or a redhead, and it certainly does have its time and place. But do me a favor and try on some navy where you would be wearing black. Then tell me you don't see a difference. (Seriously, email or tweet me—this is a challenge I will happily accept!)

Navy is just a much more flattering dark neutral for a blonde. It acts as a black without *being* a black, creating a subdued palette that is one important degree warmer—a very, very good thing for a blonde who may be washed out by the harsh intensity of black. A blonde in navy is also such a classic, stylish look—there's something about navy that will always look expensive to me. And if that blonde is blue- or green-eyed, all the better—navy will pop her eyes while warming up her skin tone.

Next, allow me to make my case for camel—oh, how I love a blonde in camel. You may think of camels, beiges, and taupes as forgettable neutrals, but on you, they are anything but. A camel can be as impactful on a blonde as a jewel tone is on a brunette, bringing out the highlights in your hair and creating the kind of harmonious picture that puts *you* at center stage. It's all about context and harmony—while beiges certainly do read as quiet in and of themselves, on a blonde they are a quiet that commands attention.

Why? Because with blondes, particularly when they're on the paler side, it's all about making sure that the colors and patterns don't overwhelm their naturally soft and subdued palette. You want to make sure that your clothes aren't wearing you, which is also the reason a bold, graphic pattern can sometimes be a mistake. Because the contrast between your hair and skin is naturally low, a very strong pattern can create an imbalance that causes your features to recede. (A dark-haired brunette with very defined eyelashes and eyebrows, on the other hand, is a natural study in strong contrasts—so when she wears a bold pattern, there is balance between the contrast in her hair and skin and the contrasting colors in her clothing.) This is a pretty subtle point, and one of the ways in which I most often see blondes go wrong. A bold pattern may not necessarily look *bad* on you, but it will read as much more of a statement—sometimes to the detriment of your presence—than it does on a brunette.

I always love a blonde in blues and greens, particularly if she's got blue or green eyes. Pop those peepers, and you'll always look like something. It really is stunning to see how dramatically a dose of sky blue right by the face can actually seem to change the color of eyes, making them appear more intense and vibrant.

As you can see if you turn to the color primer in the color insert, your color wheelhouse is not limited to neutrals or pastels—it definitely does include those bright pop colors, along with a lovely selection of peaches and earth tones.

Caviar (Classic Brunettes)

Whether your skin tone is light or dark, your shock of dark hair makes a powerful statement. That's why your color swatches are dominated by big, bold colors that stand out next to your supersaturated strands. If there is anyone who needs to get over a fear of color, it is you. Your dark hair gives you the presence to stand up to bright colors—so embrace your ability to wear attention-getting hues that would be overpowering for other women. On you, they will create harmony where they might create a choppy or severe look for a blonde.

On the other hand, where it's a powerful color for a blonde, on you, beige can be Washout City. Unless you have fairly dark skin, the wrong beige will blend in with your skin tone to create an unflattering nude look that is overpowered by the darkness of your hair and brows. For you, gray or black are much better neutrals, as is a stark white—they play off the natural contrasts in your palette, popping your dark hair and letting your features shine through. In fact, there's nothing I love more than a brunette in black and white. It always looks current, clean, and polished, presenting a study in contrast that allows the brunette's hair and features to shine through.

Brunettes do tend to have a larger latitude on the color wheel, though they need to proceed with the utmost care when it comes to pastels. Much better for you are the saturated jewel tones that match the intensity of your strands. Bold colors and patterns are your friends, and you should wear them with impunity.

When it comes to color, African-American women and Latina women may be the luckiest in all the land. Though obviously your skin comes in every shade of the rainbow, the more saturated its hue, the more leeway you have. Pigment equals presence, which means you can wear just about anything—even experimenting with neons without fear. You look just as great in jewel tones as you do in the pastels that would be murder on light-skinned brunettes, and you can often wear those beiges and camels and khakis that would wash them out as well.

Copper (Chestnuts and Redheads)

As many of you may already know, redheads need to proceed with the utmost care when it comes to color. Unlike blondes and brunettes, their hair will never read as a neutral, and so always needs to be taken into consideration. But when a redhead truly understands what colors look great on her, she will be able to use her unique gift to greatest effect. A redhead who dresses in the right colors will always be noticeable.

As with blondes (if not more so), the first thing the milk-pale redhead needs to do is ditch most of the black in her closet and swap it out for navy. In addition to warming up her skin, blue has the advantage of being a near-complementary hue to red on the color wheel, which is why it looks so great next to her hair.

Dominated by an army of chocolates, corals, peachy oranges, and blue-greens, the redhead's palette contains a deliciously saturated mix of earth tones and brighter hues. Like the blonde, she looks divine in a camel, and better in a cream than in a stark white; unlike blondes, however, redheads don't fare so well in pastels—her saturated hair will overpower those very light colors unless they are neutrals like cream or camel.

Why do redheads look so terrific in green? Because green and red are true complementary colors, hues that lie on opposite ends of the spectrum and thus present the strongest possible contrast when juxtaposed. When you want to be noticed, *wear green* (especially if your eyes are green). Or go for a unilateral color statement and paint the town red. When it's the right shade, red on a redhead can be shocking—in a very good way.

The redhead's palette also applies to the chestnut or golden-brown haired brunettes, drawing out their reddish lowlights to advantage.

Silver (and Dirty Blondes and Platinums, Too)

I love the confidence of a woman who wears her silver hair (immaculately kept, of course) with pride. I love it even more when that woman recognizes that her changing hair color means she must become increasingly attuned to her overarching color message.

The best colors for gray hair are muted, slightly grayed-out iterations of the color spectrum. While color is extremely important for my silver-haired clients—as, increasingly, are the quality of the fabric and the fit—it must be toned down in order to match the diminished intensity of the hair follicle. Think slate blues, grays, silvers, sea-foam greens, lavenders, taupes, and the like. (Red

Your Very Best Colors

Welcome to the wonderful world of color! In the following pages, I'm going to introduce you to the colors that work best for you—the shades that make you look healthier and more alive, the hues that allow *you* to shine. This simple system is based on hair color, the first stop in determining your overarching palette; but again, because skin tone is so individual and so highly variable, you'll need to experiment to see what looks best on you.

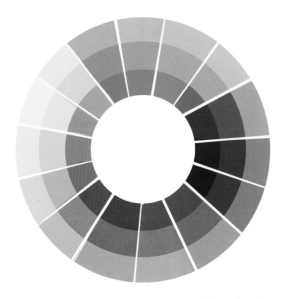

Here it is, the full color spectrum in all its glory!
Pair colors that lie at opposite ends of the wheel for the most
contrast and pop.

Honey

A Palette for All Blondes

peach

cream

navy blue

butter yellow

rose

brick red

kelly green

indigo

lavender

turquoise

camel

periwinkle

The key with blondes is to avoid overwhelming your potentially delicate palette. That doesn't mean strong colors are out—you just need to make sure they're the *right* colors. Major takeaway: Swap out the black for navy when you can.

Caviar

A Palette for Classic Brunettes

sunset red *gray* *magenta* *royal blue*

sky blue *charcoal* *lemon yellow* *pink*

blush *plum* *burnt sienna* *chestnut*

*W*hen it comes to brunettes, bright and saturated colors rule your roost. Beware of pastels (think jewel tones), and choose your light neutrals with care. Stark white or gray will generally treat you far better than beige.

Copper

A Palette for Redheads

and Tawny Brunettes

auburn   *mahogany*   *olive green*   *teal*

cerulean   *gold*   *pumpkin*   *chocolate*

crimson   *tomato red*   *pine green*   *vanilla*

Your super-saturated follicles mean you need to be extra careful with color—but they also give you room to play. Draw attention to that gorgeous mane of yours whenever you can, whether via contrast (green or blue on red) or through a monochrome approach (red or burgundy on red).

Silver

*A Palette for Silver, White,
and Salt-and-Pepper Hair*

white   *silver*   *midnight blue*

carnation pink   *onyx*   *blue green*

violet   *mint green*   *cornflower blue*

gunmetal gray   *canary yellow*   *grape*

As your hair color becomes more muted, you'll want
to do one of two things: Either wear bright colors to cast
light on your face or highlight those beautiful silver strands
by wearing complementary hues like metallics or gray.

is an exception to this rule, because it is such a pure color and one that happens to look fantastic with gray.) Beware of an overabundance of black, and embrace navy—as with the blondes and redheads, black risks overpowering you and washing you out. White, however, is fair game, and silver hair against a crisp white shirt is a lovely sight indeed.

As they enter their fifties, sixties, and beyond, some women tend to opt for a wardrobe that is increasingly classic and restricted in its colors—a uniform of dark trousers and gorgeously immaculate white blouses, for example. I understand the instinct, one that boils down style to its essentials and prizes quality and form over all else. It can be a very powerful look. But I do still advocate including a pop of color, that touch that is going to make your outfit not only classic, but also memorable. If you're looking to pare down your colors as you enter this new stage in your life, consider the power of the well-placed accessory—adding a little bit of delight, a jaunty wink in the form of a bright red cuff, a smart turquoise-rimmed pair of eyeglasses, or a charming pair of little orange flats.

A note to you bottle-dyed platinum girls and dirty blondes: You may be surprised to find yourselves in this category, but if you think about it, it makes sense—as opposed to the classic blonde's golden yellow strands, true platinum is defined by an absence of color, reading almost as white. Even if it does have a yellowish cast, the hue is so light as to "read" as white in terms of the overall contrast it creates. Platinum blondes and dirty blondes should also take a look at the colors on the blonde spectrum, however, as there will be some overlap.

The Famous Pop of Color

To layer an impactful shot of color into your wardrobe, you don't need to start swathing your entire body in bolts of neon. Strategically applied, a little bit of color can go a long way. Allow me to introduce the famous pop of color, one of my signature moves as a stylist and the reason my stylist alter ego is named "Poppa Color."

A dash of brightness on an otherwise neutral or dark outfit, the pop of color is the bold, stylish wink that mindfully applies the most vibrant of colors in the most grown-up and sophisticated of ways. It's the punctuation of a fuchsia scarf over a slate-gray blouse, or the black dress made festive with bold red shoes and bracelets.

Drawing attention to you while still allowing *you* to shine through, the pop of color takes a singular approach that makes the bright color stand out all the more against its sober backdrop. Think of menswear, and the way a dapper gentleman might wear a dark suit but pop a vibrant color by way of tie, pocket square, or socks. There's a knowing wink in wearing color this way, a restrained subtlety that says, "I don't need your attention—but I've got it, haven't I?" It's a look that communicates a certain care, a level of calculation that is appealing in its formality. You didn't just throw on a turquoise shirt—you thought about the details.

This is a way of dressing that draws the eye by way of contrast, which can be a subtler and more complex statement than an overall big, bold, and vivid approach. It's a great starting point for those who are afraid of color: Begin by using color as an accent in your tops, shoes, and accessories, and work your way up to pants, dresses, and colorful pieces of outerwear as you get more comfortable.

For many of us, color pops are also going to be a more budget-friendly way to incorporate color into our wardrobes—especially if you're about to make an investment in the solid array of well-tailored basics I outlined in the last chapter. If the bulk of your closet is composed of end-lessly mixable darks and neutrals, you can layer in the somewhat less versatile pops of color by way of items like shirts, scarves, belts, accessories, and shoes without too much of an impact on your wallet. These color pops will actually help you get the most bang out of your investment pieces, offering ways to style those basics so that they look completely different day to day. And they're great impulse buys, because you don't have to think too hard about exactly what they'll match with. Just pop a color on a dark or neutral outfit and you're good to go!

The Power of Going Monochromatic

On the opposite end of the scale lies the monochromatic outfit, an ensemble made up of pieces that are all in the same color, but not necessarily of the same color "value." A monochromatic outfit based on khaki might include cream and brown—all three are lighter or darker shades in the same color family.

A great way to make separates look like they were born to be worn together, it's a look that can be very under-stated and elegant. Though it works best when the fabrics are lush and the clothing is of high quality, a monochromatic statement can also make inexpensive outfits look positively luxe. It's most often used with neutrals, but it can also be done with vivid colors for a bold approach that commands attention.

When you're going monochromatic, think of using texture or metallics in the same way you would pop a color. So an all-gray outfit could be popped with a sequined tank, or even a silk tank whose sheen acts as the "pop." The goal is to make sure that there is enough variation in your outfit—whether that variation comes from hue or fabric— that you're not creating an indistinguishable mass.

Your Color Soul Mate

Here's a great shortcut to finding your power colors—pick a TV personality whose look you like and who has a hair and skin tone similar to yours. Anyone who regularly appears on TV has had their colors chosen by a stylist and an army of advisors with the care and strategy of a general planning a war. So pay attention to what they have on, and try out those colors for yourself—if it looks fantastic on Katie or Oprah, odds are it might look great on you, too.

How to Wear Black

The first thing to know about black is that it is an extremely powerful color. The purest of statements, the essence of simplicity, it is a hue so saturated and severe that it eliminates all distraction, concentrating attention on the essential qualities of a garment—its fit, its shape, its drape, its fabric—and on the personality of the wearer. Black carves out a negative space around whomever it clothes, allowing her face, silhouette, and exposed flesh to stand out as if held under a spotlight. Sexy, edgy, and mysterious, it is the cover of night, the urban armor we wear when the stakes are high, the elegant uniform with which we adorn ourselves when the occasion calls for glamour and class. Not to mention its unequaled power to slim and trim, magically shaving away inches like a monthlong trip to a serious boot camp (minus the extreme pain and suffering).

Although once canonized by the likes of Coco Chanel as the epitome of chic, the color black has since been demoted to a thoughtless neutral of the modern age. I want to take back the color black and save it from its bum rap. So, for a start, here's how *not* to wear black. Black is not a neutral to be worn as a go-anywhere, statement-free hodgepodge of textures, fabrics, and shapes. Black is not to be worn as a respite from effort or as a cloak of invisibility.

Yet all too often, it is. Worn as a cop-out, a faded cardigan tossed over a pair of stretched-out yoga pants, black has become a messy garbage bag we throw over our bodies on those days when we don't feel like trying, when we're hoping to fade into the background. But remember, *hiding is not living.* (Nor is it effective—as I've said, when we use color, fabric, or shape to hide, we only draw attention to our own discomfort.) And using black as a color in which to hide does a disservice to its natural elegance and overall excellence.

Black can be an *amazing* color, but as with everything you put on your body, it will only work for you when it is worn with intention. One of the main points I want to get across to you in this book is that there are no loopholes. There are no "statement-free" outfits, and that goes for the color black as much as for anything else.

In fact, because it is so streamlined and so intensely saturated, if anything black is a color that requires *more* consciousness on the part of the wearer, and that requires more from the garment itself. The way I see it, your black clothing should be (or look) expensive—because when it isn't, it is likely to read as shabby.

Wearing Your "Off" Colors

Though in an ideal world, you'd never be wearing a less-than-flattering color next to your face, I get that there are times when it's unavoidable. Maybe you already own several otherwise great investment pieces in slightly off colors that are not necessarily the most becoming but aren't egregious enough to warrant total banishment. Maybe you've been chosen as a bridesmaid in your best friend's wedding and are going to be stuck in an unflattering mint green. (Thanks, friend!)

In these cases, look to makeup and jewelry to skew the balance. If you love a particular piece that you know isn't one of your best colors, make sure you pop the lipstick (one of the fastest ways to make a big color statement on your face) that both flatters your skin tone and complements the garment. You can also do this with jewelry, pumping up a duller top with a big, bright, and vibrant necklace.

As you're developing your awareness of the entirety of your color message, be sure that includes your face as well.

When you are tired and feel like hiding (and if trying to do a mood turnaround by draping yourself in bright colors is out of the question), throw on a soft, light color in a luxurious fabric that makes you feel coddled and cared for. A neutral can be quiet without being severe—dark colors can be murder next to an overtired face.

Black can, however, be a great base from which to pop a color, a look I love. Popping a vibrant color on a black outfit will always look elegant, modern, and put-together. It creates a vivid, highly visible contrast that practically drips with confidence, letting everyone know that you are *not* afraid of being noticed (and for all the right reasons).

Metals and Minerals: Your Jewelry and Makeup

When it comes to the jewelry, the classic WASP look may be a simple silver watch (along with a pair of diamond studs and, of course, a giant rock). But to me, blondes actually look best in gold. Gold is the metal that brings out the highlights in your hair and the warmth in your skin, and I really want my blondes to sparkle. Same goes for redheads—I love the way it picks up the warm tones in their hair and skin. Though brunettes can look great in gold, I tend to prefer them in silver; the contrast between silver and a thick mane of dark hair reads like the contrast between white and black. It's a stronger and thus more impactful juxtaposition.

In the end it will all depend on your particular skin tone, so find out for yourself: Put on a white tee, grab some silver and gold jewelry, and check it out in the mirror against a white background. Which metal makes your skin look healthier? That's your ticket. (You may look equally great in both.)

Makeup is an epic color story of its own, which is why I strongly urge you to go in for a professional consultation if you've never had one before. It's a treat, and you'll learn a whole bunch of great tips. (Be sure to make the most of your glam moment by scheduling a night out afterward!)

In general, you want your eye makeup to be doing one of two things: either popping your peepers by way of contrast or intensifying their hue by mirroring it. An example of the first would be a brown shadow on blue eyes. If you look at the color wheel in the color insert, you'll see that those two colors are near opposites on the spectrum; when set side by side, they create a bold, attention-getting contrast.

When it comes to the lips, it's all about finding those reds, pinks, plums, and corals that work for your complexion so that you can mix and match depending on what you are wearing. You never want too much color on your face, so do heed the tried-and-true makeup artist's tip of focusing on either the eyes or the lip.

Pulling It All Together

Now that you've begun to get a sense of the colors with which you should be experimenting, it's time to consider the way you will be pulling all this information into a single harmonious message. The first thing to know is that there are no hard-and-fast rules when it comes to color. Color is a trick of light, an ever-changing master of illusion that shape-shifts depending on the environment in which it is seen and the hues beside which it appears. Color is *always* seen in context.

Again, we're getting into some advanced territory here, but I want to give you a broad sense of how changeable color truly is. Though we've identified the colors that work best for you, color is not a static language—everything depends on how those hues are deployed, which is why you always need to take a step back and evaluate the palette of your ensembles in the here and now.

To that end, here are three ways to evaluate the context of your color scheme:

1. **Consider your overarching message.** Due to a visual phenomenon that color experts call "simultaneous contrast," our perceptions of a particular color can actually shift depending on the colors with which it is seen. Colors at opposite ends of the color spectrum will pump each other up the most—red and green, or black and white for instance—while colors that are very close to each other on the color wheel create a subtler contrast. Take a look at which colors lie opposite one another on the color wheel in the color insert if you're curious about how this works, and know that you have the power to bump up or tone down a color's vibrancy depending on what you wear with it. Play with it and see.

2. **Consider the garment.** How a color is perceived also depends on the style of the garment it graces. While a brown sweater may pair well with black leggings and brown riding boots, a flirty brown dress with a sexy low-cut back may look dull when paired with black shoes; with that flirty dress, a pair of gold strappy heels would up the ante and round out the playful, sexy mes-

sage. Make sure your overall color message is consistent with the style of the garment.

3. Consider the environment. While a black blazer over a silver tank and jeans may look great against New York's cool eastern light and steely skyscrapers, such an ensemble may read as harsh in the bright light of Los Angeles, with its coastal landscape and vivid sunsets. Color cannot stand apart from the environment and culture in which it is seen, or from the overall palette of which it is a part.

Control the Message

Your color makeover began with the act of finding out which colors flattered you—and now that we've identified these colors, we're going to learn how to use them to your advantage.

Fundamentally, it all comes back to the question "What does it say?" This is the question I want you to be asking of everything you put on your body—and that includes the color of your clothing, one of the most powerful ways in which our clothing "speaks" for us.

Because of color's deep and often mysterious power to transmit mood and emotion, the psychology of color is big business. Corporations pay consultants to help them figure out which colors are going to keep their employees happiest, and politicians and other public figures spend big bucks and countless hours trying to determine which hues are going to win them the most votes and help them make the most of their airtime. All the while, trend experts determine which colors are going to be the "it" hues every year, and designers place big bets on their findings.

You could easily get lost in this sea of opinions, counter-opinions, and ever-changing trends, but it's really not so complicated as it seems. If you think about color in general terms (warm versus cool, bright versus muted, dark versus light), you'll be well on your way.

To start you off, here are some simple, can't-miss guidelines to matching your colors to the outcomes you desire:

- When you want to appear warm and inviting, wear light-colored neutrals like white, cream, or camel—they're accessible without making specific statements—or warm up a darker palette by throwing in a light-colored neutral. Great examples of circumstances in which you'd want your outfit to say "warm and inviting" include a meeting in which you hold the upper hand and want to put the other parties at ease; anytime you are hosting people in your home; and first dates.

▪ For a look that is cheerful, fun, and perky, wear warm and bright colors. Think coral, grass green, peach, or lemon yellow. We are generally attracted to people who seem positive and happy, so looking cheerful and happy can be just as much of a power move as it is a mood booster to you and those around you. Unless you're going on an early date (in which case you'd want to either amp up the sex appeal or go for a more neutral color statement) or heading to a very high-stakes meeting, I say you can never go wrong with a little bit of cheer.

▪ Want to exude drama and sex appeal? Go for dark colors, red (the sexpot's classic hue of choice), vibrant jewel tones, or neutrals with metallic or sheen. Black is always mysterious, sexy, and slimming. Sequins and silks draw the eye by capturing the light, turning you into the beautiful focal point of your suitor's attentions.

■ When it comes to communicating power, it's all about the context. In the right context, bright orange could be a power move. (Think bold silk blouse under a navy blazer—the classic pop of color.) Black can also be a very powerful color, as can red or purple. (Again, think of those politicians and their red ties or of royalty's trademark hue.) But to my mind, the most powerful colors are those colors that "pop" your features and make the most of your natural assets. On a blonde, cream or camel could be a power color—though it's considered anything but. On a brunette, black and white can be very striking, and patterns can be used to calculating effect. It all comes back to knowing your colors (turn to the color primer in the color insert for a reminder), and understanding the intrinsic message a particular garment puts out.

the compact of truth

a color assessment

We're not going to take a deep dive into your current wardrobe yet—that's just ahead in the next chapter—but for the sake of a color assessment I do want you to take an initial spin through your closet so that you get a sense of what your default, unconscious palette looks like. This will be easy enough to do at a glance, without rummaging through your drawers or even taking anything off its hanger. Just take a look around and see what leaps out at you. Keep your notebook by your side in case any epiphanies should happen to emerge, and consider the following questions:

- What is the dominant palette in your closet? A sea of beige, black, brown? An uncategorizable, frenetic mix? Once you've identified the reigning hues, ask yourself what it is that attracts you to these colors. Fear of color? Force of habit? A desire for invisibility? A mistaken idea about what looks best on you?

■ How do these colors make you feel? If the answer is anything less than "great," we've got some work to do. Are you excited by the colors in your closet? Is there delight to be found in there? There should be!

■ Does your closet contain a solid dose of the colors that look best on you? Check out the palettes in the color insert and make note of some of the colors you'd like to experiment with.

■ Which colors in your closet currently garner you the most compliments? It's important to take note of this because we often undervalue the color knowledge we already have. I've had clients say things like "Oh yeah, I know that color looks really good on me" about a color that is represented only once or twice in their wardrobe. Hello! If a color looks amazing on you, there is no shame in stocking up on that color and wearing the heck out of it. People won't think of you as the girl who's always wearing green—they'll think of you as the girl who always looks great!

- What are the colors you live in every day? Be honest with yourself about what you actually wear. I often see clients whose closets are filled with aspirational colors. They may be attracted to big, bold colors but tend to leave them hanging in their closets, gravitating by force of habit to the duller ends of the spectrum. Are you wearing the color in the closet, or just letting it take up space? Why is this? Working with color can take a bit more effort. Are you sticking to neutrals because you find them easier to work with? Or are you waiting for the right mood to strike? Mistake! Don't wait for the colorful mood to find you—color can actually change your mood, thereby altering the outcome of your day.

- What are the intimidatingly vivid colors you tend to wear only for special occasions, if at all? Think about what it would take for you to wear these colors more regularly. Do you just need to take the leap, or are you missing the right neutrals with which to pair these colorful pieces? If you can identify a piece or two you think might help you get more wear out of the color in your closet—whether it's a nude heel, a navy blazer, or the right trench coat—make a note. If not, don't worry—by the end of this book you will know exactly what you need.

Color is complicated, and some of us are naturally great at it; others less so. If you fall into the latter category, the good news is that you have plenty of tools at your disposal. If you find yourself falling into a color rut, check my Pinterest page to see collections of my favorite looks for Honeys, Caviars, Coppers, and Silvers. If you're seeing a trend color everywhere you go but can't figure out how to work with it, odds are pretty good that it will be featured in an extensive how-to in a current issue of your fashion magazine of choice. And if you've purchased a new item whose color has you feeling unsure, ask Rent-a-George or a trusted friend for an opinion. Sometimes we are too blinded by our attraction to a particular garment to be honest with ourselves about whether it really is doing anything for us. A true friend will always tell you.

chapter 5

the purge
taming your closet

Have nothing in your house that you do not know to be useful, or believe to be beautiful.

—William Morris

Tell me everything . . . about your closet. What's the first thing that comes up for you when you picture it in your mind's eye? Excitement? A sense of possibility and play? A feeling of confidence and empowerment?

More likely, your closet is a bit of a black hole you'd really rather *not* have to consider at all. But that's exactly what we're going to do. In this chapter, we are going to dive in, braving even the deepest, darkest recesses of that small, hidden room as we get down to the serious business of closet cleaning. It's going to be *so* worth it. At the end of this process, you're going to have a beautifully clean and organized closet that is devoid of what I call "clunkers"—those clothes that are not doing anything for you except weighing you down.

The sorting process is likely to be a learning experience, and in a *huge* way. Finding out what's really hiding in that cave of yours will give you an invaluable bird's-eye view on the true state of your wardrobe, and it will provide clues as to how you got into your current fix.

The closet is the place where our interactions with the outside world begin. In order to change what we project— and, in turn, what we manifest in our lives—we must start from the inside out. We must begin by confronting your closet, finding out what's really in there, and yes, letting go of some serious baggage.

The Master Cleanse

Ever been around anyone who's done a master cleanse? Then I'm guessing you're familiar with the master cleanser's tendency to go on and on (and on) about how *great* it is to starve yourself half to death and how *amazing* the high is—if you can just make it to the twenty-seventh liquid meal. Well, it is your turn to get back at all of the juicers in your life, because once you go through your full-throttle closet purge, you are going to be singing the praises of your new, unencumbered lifestyle from the rooftops. And the best part? No maple-syrup lemon-juice cayenne-peppered "meals" in sight.

The closet purge should be an incredibly centering and calming process. It's powerful. Clearing your wardrobe of what's essentially trash rids you of the burden of daily Dumpster-diving and allows you to take a true inventory of what you have, and what you need.

Can you imagine a world in which you love everything in your closet? That world is absolutely within reach. But first, you're going to have to get rid of those hideous cargo capri pants and that prom dress you still wear to the annual office holiday party.

This isn't about chucking everything you own. There are gems in that closet of yours—and we're going to find them and make sure they are shined up and polished (read: properly tailored, styled, and accessorized) so that they feature you at your best. As we go, we will be putting together a list of what's missing. Would those houndstooth slacks that fit you so well look better with a flowy silk blouse and a soft little cardie than a faded, stretched-out black tee? (The answer is *yes*.) But if the fit isn't right, out the door they will go.

Since I'm not going to be there with you to hear your responses and take you through the process—though I so, so wish I could be!—I highly recommend you invite Rent-a-George over to help you out. In fact, this may be the most important piece of his very illustrious job. An objective set of eyes will help you get the job done in around three hours (as opposed to three days) and make it lots more fun, too.

Reading Your Closet

What does your closet say about you? What is the story that it tells about your life? Is it a story you want to be living, a story that is true to your personality, your goals and aspirations? Or does it tell a story that was accurate ten or twenty years ago but is no longer true? When we hold on to clothes for too long, we may be holding on to a life stage we have passed through—this is why it's so important to do a periodic cleanse. I see it in so many of my clients: the closetful of cheap frilly dresses and odd flea-market finds that may have worked just fine for a twenty-something barista but aren't such a good match for a thirty-something professional. Or the closetful of newly purchased, never-worn mistakes with the tags still attached. (The more recent the error, the more difficult it may be to let it go—but if these purchases have nothing to do with who you are or how you want the world to see you, they must be taken to the curb.)

The closet is the place where your inner world meets the outside world, the place where you enact a crucial transition from private to public. Its state is a *gigantic* clue as to how you feel not only about your clothes, but also about what you're projecting to the outside world. What are you hiding in there? Does it look like a down-at-the-heels thrift shop, full of dust-covered heaps of clothes you've been meaning to mend for years, creased shoes, hardened belts, pilled sweaters, frayed jackets with balding cuffs, and ten-year-old skirts that have never been worn? What does that communicate, and how does it affect your everyday life? Again, there may be gems hiding in that mountain of stuff that doesn't fit, flatter, or project the right image. But wading through a garbage heap of sidelined garments every morning is a whole lot of work, both on a psychic level and in terms of sheer time.

If you're worried that a closet cleanse is going to leave you high and dry with nothing to put on your body, I'll let you in on a secret: The odds are pretty high that you are already wearing what you feel and look good in anyway. Having been a guest inside countless closets, I can pretty much guarantee you this: Seventy percent of what's in your closet is just not being worn. Sound crazy? Let's take a good hard look inside . . .

The Case for the Perfect 10

I'm going to go ahead and repeat one of my favorite axioms: *Everything in your closet should be a 10*. Every single thing that you put on your body, whether it's shoes, loungewear, everyday pants, jeans, dressy tees, structured shifts and blazers, or that pull-out-all-the-stops cocktail dress, should be an irrefutable 10. That means it's got to be the right color for you, the right fit for you, the right style for you, and the right message for you to be putting out at this stage in your life. You deserve nothing less.

How do you know when it's a 10?

You know. You just do. When you put it on and feel great and want to twirl around in front of the mirror, that's a 10. When you get compliments on it, that's a 10, too. When it's the right color, the right fit, the right style for you, that's a 10.

A 10 doesn't have to mean a runway-ready event outfit or a high-powered suit. It could mean a cashmere sweater in the right color for your hair and skin tone, a skinny jean, and a little bootie, or even jeans and a tank top with a cheerful zip-up hoodie in one of your signature colors. A 10 is an item that not only makes you feel great, but also signals your sense of self-worth to the world. Why would you settle for anything less? We attract what we put out, so go out there and get after it.

Tales from the Crypt

From the looks of her closet, you'd have thought Anna, a nutritionist in her forties, was planning on opening up a thrift shop of her own—not one of those consignment shops with gorgeous vintage picks, but more of a buy-by-the-pound (and then wish you hadn't) kind of store.

A gorgeously statuesque woman with a great figure and loads of personality, Anna had a style situation so dire that even her doting husband was itching to get in on the action. (Ladies, when your husband begs a stylist to *please help his wife into some decent clothes*, it's time to let this loving man have his intervention!)

What I found in her closet: an *insane* cacophony of fabrics, textures, colors, and shapes that had absolutely nothing to do with her lifestyle, body type, coloring, or personality; a mind-blowing number of turtlenecks; and a colorful assortment of spandex hoochie dresses. You heard me right: Her closet's schizophrenic rainbow spanned blocky cotton turtlenecks (likely to be paired with jeans and loafers), spandex, and prairie skirts—don't even get me started on the footwear she paired with those.

When we dug a little deeper, we found sweaters with built-in shoulder pads *from the eighties*. Look, I know we've been in the midst of an eighties revival for quite some time now, but for those of you who aren't geniuses in the math department, please allow me to spell it out: She was holding on to sweaters she'd had for thirty years. Thirty years!

Like every woman I've ever met, Anna is a multifaceted individual. One part of her is conservative, serious, and grown-up—and another Anna is ready to get down, hit the club, and turn a few heads while she's at it. I repeat: turtlenecks and hoochie dresses! In all seriousness, this is an issue I see with so many of the women I work with. They think of their "everyday" clothes as "basics"—by which they mean a category that doesn't have to look much like anything, because all it does is serve the function of . . . *being worn every day*.

Do you see what I'm getting at here?

Don't get into the mind-set of saving up all the sexy and fabulous stuff for those nights out with the girls! First of all, I feel sorry for the rest of your days. Second, you're going to be so starved for the sexy on those nights out that you're likely to overcompensate—going from turtlenecks to hoochie dresses in a transformation so drastic it breeds an air of inauthenticity and desperation. Your authentic self inhabits a place somewhere in between Eskimo and pole dancer. Let's find a way to dress that is going to seamlessly express all these variations without making you look like you've jumped off the crazy train or are trying to become something you're not.

Yes, No, Maybe So

With our George by our side and our pen and notebook
at the ready, into the closet we go. Where to begin? Don't
overthink it. We're eventually going to be sifting through
your whole wardrobe piece by piece, from your jeans,
tees, and dresses to your coats, shoes, and yes, even belts,
bags, and jewelry. Every single thing that you put on your
body is about to undergo a serious level of scrutiny, so
it doesn't much matter where you begin. Left to right,
or right to left—choose your method. If you've already
got your clothing sorted by season, you can opt to focus
on only the current stuff and save the rest of the year for
a second go-round; in fact, I recommend this approach,

because it means your fashion to-do list won't be left hanging around like a sad sack for a full season while you lose all of the great momentum and urgency that originally inspired your purge.

If you don't yet have your closet sorted seasonally, here's a wonderful opportunity to rectify this egregious wrong. The fewer off-season clothes you confront each morning, the greater your odds of composing a gorgeous and seasonally appropriate ensemble. The simple act of seasonal sorting can itself be transformative, allowing you to truly see what you're contending with and providing you with a better sense of what's missing (or of what's all-too-present) in your closet. You may be blind to the fact that while you have sixteen sweaters for winter, you only have three workable tank tops for summer—until you can see the opposing piles undeniably stacked up. So before you and George get going, sort your wardrobe into two sections: spring and summer, and winter and fall. (Don't let yourself fall into a seasonal identity crisis over those transitional items—just lump them into the current season.) This should be a relatively quick and painless process, as it doesn't involve any value judgments.

Once your closet is split in half, I do recommend going through an entire season in one cathartic and gigantically productive session—but I *have* had clients tell me that they'd cleaned out their closets over a period of weeks. If the task of sorting through a season's worth of clothing seems unmanageable, this slow-food approach can be a great way to overcome emotional attachment. While you may not be able to let go of an item right off the bat, trying on a few outfits every day after work and adding to your "No" pile little by little may make the task more manageable. It should be a lot easier to face the music after the fifth time you try on that dress that you allegedly love but haven't worn in five years.

Whichever method you choose, stay positive by keeping your eye on the big picture. Cleaning out your closet shouldn't be an exercise in self-loathing or self-blame. You will confront mistakes, but your primary goal here is not to rate yourself as a shopper and burgeoning stylist but to give yourself the gift of the wardrobe you deserve. The end point of this entire process is a closet that makes you feel and look more confident. So instead of asking yourself, "What was I thinking?" ask yourself a different question: "Does this piece of clothing make me feel great?" It should. If it doesn't, don't wear it! Give it to someone who will, or get rid of it.

The Seven Habits of Highly Effective Closets

How do you decide what to keep and what to chuck? There's no rocket science involved here, but there are no shortcuts, either. You're eventually going to be taking out every single piece in your closet, and either trying it on or holding it up to your face. You may find that you need to do more trying on at the beginning of the process, and that as you pick up speed, it becomes easier and easier to make decisions.

As you go, you'll be sorting your clothing into three piles: "Yeses," "Nos," and "Maybes." With each item, you'll want to apply the following conditions—and see whether George pipes up to corroborate your assessments:

1. IT FITS. This one might sound basic, but it's crucial. If a piece of clothing does not fit you correctly, either get it out of sight or, if it's worth it, see if you can get it altered. The same goes for an item that used to fit or almost fits. I *do not* believe in fat and skinny clothes. You have to love the body you're in, and dress the body you're in—that's absolutely, positively your best chance at making the body you have today look and feel amazing. Monthly ups and downs aside, having aspirational clothes in your closet is only going to do you a disservice, on both a practical and a psychic level. Nine times out of ten, the better your clothes fit, the better you are going to look. That doesn't mean you can't wear a slouchy sweater—it just means that you have to think about proportion. If that sweater is slouchy in a good way, can it be paired with leggings or skinny jeans and flats for a great weekend outfit?

2. IT FLATTERS. It isn't enough for something to merely fit you—it *must* (I can't stress this enough) do at least one great thing for your body and your face. First and foremost, is it the right color, a color that highlights your eyes, provides a beautiful contrast or complement to your hair, makes your skin glow with good health? Turn back to Chapter 4 and to the color primer in the color insert to check out your palette if you're unsure. Next, what does the fit *do* for you? Show off your tiny waist and great curves? Reveal the cut shoulders you've earned with all those downward-facing-dogs? You deserve more than clothes you're simply able to button, so ask yourself whether an item plays off your eye color, skin tone, hair color, and/or body type, and proceed accordingly.

3. IT'S IN GOOD SHAPE. Is it trashed and worn to death? Faded and saggy? Threadbare and moth-eaten? Time to say good-bye. I see *so* many women hanging on to clothing that's far, far too old because deep down, they fear they may never again find something they feel as comfortable in. These days there is a ton of great stuff out there for every body shape, complexion, style, and age, so there's just no excuse for dimming that beautiful light of yours by hiding in worn-out, off-color garments. A piece of clothing that is past its prime sends the same signal as a two-inch display of faded roots, telegraphing a lack of self-care that tells people you don't want to be looked at. We want you in a position to welcome any attention that comes your way.

4. IT'S NOT DATED. I'm not talking about the difference between this year's clothes and last year's. My aim isn't to have you walking the runway—I want you in the clothes that make sense for your lifestyle. But whatever your style, I also want you to look like someone who pays attention to the world around her, who isn't stuck in a time warp or wearing clothing that is just plain old. *But I'm conservative,* you're thinking. (I know you are, because it's something *so* many of my clients say.) But you can be conservative and look current at the same time—a fashion-forward accessory, top, or shoe acts much the same way as that famous pop of color, freshening up your whole look and making you a pleasure to behold.

5. YOU'VE WORN IT RECENTLY. Special-occasion garments aside, if an item is in season but hasn't been on your back in a month or longer (or ever!), you need to ask yourself *why.* I'm pretty sure you can come up with the answer. Is it unflattering, in poor condition, or out of style? That's a dead ringer for the "No" pile. Is it a solid item, but one you've never been able to figure out how to wear? Think about what you'd need in order to pull together a great outfit, and whip out that to-do list.

6. WEARING IT MAKES YOU FEEL GOOD. Notice what happens to your posture when you put on an item of clothing. Do you shrink up, all wrapped up in your cardigan like a tiny wallflower, or do you instinctively slip into a power pose? Pay attention to your body language—it can sometimes speak more clearly than your conscious mind allows. When you're considering an item you wear all the time, don't accept its presence in your closet just because it's "in the rotation." Let's go deeper. When you have it on, how do you feel? Do you receive compliments about the way you look in it? Remember, we are going for nothing less than a closet full of 10s here.

7. WHAT DOES IT SAY? Again, you should be able to answer this question about every single piece in your closet— the answers will enable you to use your wardrobe to impact every single situation in your life. If a particular item has you stumped, then ask yourself where you would wear the item, and why. If you're still having trouble, pretend it's part of a costume. Who would wear this costume? Is this a character you're comfortable playing?

That may seem like a whole lot of dialogue, but in reality it will all take place very quickly. You shouldn't spend more than a couple of minutes, max, on any item—indecision is what "Maybe" piles are for.

If something doesn't look good, take the time to ask yourself why. This is a learning opportunity. Take that dress that you love but that's always made you feel slightly bigger than you really are. What exactly is so off about it? Sometimes, all we need to do is ask the question and the answer will pop right up. Maybe the straps are set too far apart and make you look like you don't have much of a shoulder. On the flip side, why are the clothes that do work so flattering? Figure out the whys, and you'll soon have a customized set of rules for foolproof, clunker-free shopping.

Excuses, Excuses

Inside each of us lies a quiet little hoarder. She's strong-willed, sentimental, and suffers from a severe attachment disorder. It can be very hard for her to let things go, so don't be surprised if she pipes up during your closet purge. Here are some of the things I've heard her say:

"I just wear that when I'm running around town." Last time I checked, "town" was a public space through which other people tend to roam. What happens if you bump into someone you know when you're "running around" in your ex-boyfriend's holey sweats and his yellowed, ill-fitting tee? And more important, what happens when you run into someone you *don't* know? Will that sexy off-duty fireman take a gander at you in such an outfit? Doubtful.

"Oh yeah, I *know*, my mom gave me that." I have a question. Does your mother accompany you on dates or to the office? If so, we've got bigger fish to fry. I am so very sorry to have to break this to your mom, but she just doesn't get to dress her adult daughter. I do think it's acceptable for you to hang on to one or two pieces out of familial obligation, provided they are not so unflattering you can't pull them out for the occasional Christmas dinner, but the rest of the stuff has got to go. It's just taking up room in your closet and making it harder for you to see the great stuff that's hiding in there. (If she would like to discuss this further, please tell your mother to feel free to give me a call—I am very good with mothers!)

"That's what I throw on when I'm walking the dog." Have you ever watched a romantic comedy? Walking the dog is screenwriter's code for "Great time to meet someone!" Single or not, dog-walking is prime time for socializing. Dogs are essentially accessories we use to sniff out other like-minded humans—woof!

"But it was only ten dollars!" I don't have anything against cheap clothes, and I love a deal as much as you do, but I don't want you choking your closet with spur-of-the-moment bargains. Putting the brakes on some of that impulse buying will enable you to get some things you actually look great in. I'm all for inexpensive stuff, but I want it to be thoughtful, flattering, and appropriate to the life you want to be living.

"I could never get rid of that—it still fits/has sentimental value." I hear this one more often than you'd think, and it's usually applied to clothing that is *vintage*, but not in a good way—we're talking about stuff that's been hanging around since the tenth grade. Yes, it *is* wonderful that that black velvet Esprit jacket circa 1992 has survived the test of time. We'll give it an extra-nice eulogy when we consecrate it to the giveaway pile—I'm sure a tenth grader somewhere will be very happy to have it.

"Those are just my gym clothes." Get ready to take a good, hard look at your gym clothes and loungewear— I see *so* many clients going to the gym in what look like house-cleaning outfits. I understand that the gym may not be your ideal social or networking environment, and that you may indeed *want* to feel invisible when you're exercising. But as I keep repeating (because it's so true!), our don't-look-at-me clothes are the ones that make us noticeable—and not in a good way. If you want to be subdued at the gym, wear a sleek, slimming, all-black outfit. That way, when someone does see you, you'll have nothing to feel ashamed of. More important, I believe that attentiveness is contagious. Pay attention to what you are putting on your body, every day and in every area of your life, with no exceptions, and that method will become automatic habit. For more on how to dress for the gym, turn back to page 94.

"Not my super-super-*super*-skinny jeans!" Fluctuating weight is a reality for many of us, and I'm not opposed to your keeping a couple of sizes in your closet to allow for those normal monthly ups and downs. But if you are holding on to jeans in every size from a two to an eight and have your closet sorted into categories like fat, sort of fat, a little bloated, skinny, oh-my-God-I-haven't-eaten-in-six-months skinny . . . I'm staging an intervention. Honoring and dressing the body you have *at this moment in time* will give you the greatest shot at looking spectacular *right now*. Those starvation-diet jeans aren't helping you out—they are emotional baggage that is weighing you down and taking up valuable space in your closet and in your psyche. Let's clear away the cobwebs and let the light shine in.

"I've been meaning to get that fixed." Really? Reality check! If an item has been sitting in your closet waiting to be taken to a tailor for six months or more, I think the odds of said item ever making it out the door in anything but a giveaway bag are pretty slim. The exception: If you are sitting on a pile of truly fabulous clothing in need of doable tweaks (rather than just putting off the act of getting rid of things you *know* you shouldn't be wearing), now is the time to get that stuff out and take the plunge. There is nothing more satisfying than taking a piece from a 7 to a 10 by nipping it in at the waist or simply hemming it to a proper length. I personally love getting things altered—it makes me feel *very* Cary Grant.

"No way—it fits!" Let's not confuse a piece of clothing that *fits* with a piece of clothing that *flatters*. Remember, we are going for a closet full of 10s. If you learn to slow down and shop with consciousness and purpose rather than in a flurry of mindless or habit-fueled acquisition, you *will* find beautiful things that fit . . . *and* flatter.

Shoes, Accessories, and Odds and Ends

As you're pulling things from your closet, you'll inevitably find yourself putting outfits together to see whether a disputed piece might be a worthwhile complement to an undisputed 10. Don't fight the urge to put on the shoes and rock the jewelry, because we're going to get there in due time anyway.

Once you've gone through all of the clothes, we're going to go through the jewelry and the shoes and the belts and the handbags with the very same zeal and attention to detail you've demonstrated thus far. These decisions tend to be easier to make, especially when it comes to irredeemably broken-down footwear and jewelry you never even liked. Doesn't that feel good?

"But I wear that *all* the time!" There it is: the number-one reason women give me for not wanting to throw something away, no matter how obviously unflattering, worn-out, or inappropriate the item. You may wear that long, sad, droopy cardigan several times a week—but *should* you? I understand how an item that, deep down, you know isn't quite right could come to feel indispensable—maybe without that cardigan, you'd lack a basic lightweight layer to throw on in your chilly office. We also tend to get emotionally attached to those clothes we wear all the time, which makes it hard for us to say good-bye. Take a deep breath. We're not going to strip you down to nothing—the goal here certainly *isn't* to have you go naked, but rather to find beautiful, flattering, and useful alternatives to the subpar pieces in your closet.

Sorting Out the Piles and Dealing with the "Maybes"

If you're still feeling some trepidation about letting things go, check back in with your emotional state midway through your closet cleanse. I won't be surprised to hear that you've taken to it like an OCD germaphobe on a spring-cleaning binge—I can't tell you how often I've seen clients take a break from manically tossing armfuls of bad jeans into the mountain of rejects on their floor to turn to me and shout, *"This feels great!"*

Once you and your George have gone through the current season of your wardrobe and sorted every last item into "Yes," "No," and "Maybe" piles, it's time to deal with that pesky last category. Go through the "Maybe" pile again, piece by piece, and try to make decisions; if you can't, at least winnow the pile down so you can come back to it later.

If you're really on the fence about a piece of clothing you think *might* work, make a mental note to take it out for a spin. Put it on, style it to the nines, and see how you feel that day. Are you basking in confidence and compliments? Sometimes all it takes is ten steps out the door for us to realize an outfit is W-R-O-N-G. And sometimes all we need to do is break through our initial discomfort at trying something different before we realize how very, very right it is. Pay attention to how you feel, and to how people respond to you. I truly believe that you already know whether it's right or not—in clothing as in all things, it's all about learning to pay attention to that inner voice.

Is attachment rearing its sweet, nostalgic head? When you're looking at a beloved item that has been with you for a long time, picture yourself passing it in a store today. Would that cap-sleeved floral dress with the sweetheart neckline still catch your eye? If you wouldn't buy it now, you shouldn't be wearing it now.

The Life Stage Test

Newsflash: The bohemian culottes you wore as a twenty-something aspiring performance artist are probably not looking so appropriate at forty. Same goes for the skin-tight dollar-store dresses you donned in your single years and the awkward suit you picked out for your very first round of job interviews. That frayed pile of Forever 21 duds? The name says it all.

Even if the traces of those bygone decades aren't as radical as the giant pair of college-era, bright purple stretch drawstring pantaloons I found in one client's closet—she claimed these were her "traveling pants"—if your style has been pretty consistent over the last ten, fifteen, or even twenty years, odds are you're in need of what I call a life stage reassessment.

So many things can change over the years. Our circumstances, our careers, our lifestyles, our bodies, our budgets. But all too often, we fail to adjust our wardrobes to suit our evolving realities. At some point, we figured out a formula we felt comfortable with. Because many of us find shopping and dressing so fraught, and because we do tend to grow so attached to our clothes, we then proceed to stick with that formula through thick and thin.

Or we allow our complex feelings about change to rule our fashion choices. Aging can be scary, and one of the ways we deal with that fear is by refusing to face it head-on. And so we ignore the changes coming over our bodies and continue to dress them in the exact same way, regardless of whether those styles are still flattering or appropriate; we gloss over the changes in our identities, failing to present ourselves in a way that aligns with the sometimes profound shifts on our personal and professional continuum.

To put it another way: If you're still dressing for the position you outgrew three promotions ago, you're probably not dressing for the job you want. And by extension, if you're dressing for a part you haven't inhabited in ten or twenty or thirty years, you're probably not dressing for the *life* you want.

When it comes to the question of aging, there're no two ways about it: You must confront the changing realities of your appearance head-on. As I've said, you are going to be seen, no matter what you do—and evaluating your appearance with a clear eye is your best insurance against being seen in a negative light.

Saying Good-bye

Don't be surprised if your "No" pile winds up filling several trash bags—I see it every single time I go through this process with my clients. What to do with the surplus? First, sort it into three or four piles: across-the-board items in great condition that you think might appeal to friends; work clothes and dress clothes in great condition; basics and outerwear in great to good to serviceable condition; anything in poor or horrible condition.

Take that last pile, divvy it up into trash bags, and take it to the garbage heap where it belongs. Better yet, if you have an incinerator, let it burn, baby, burn! No one wants your sweat-stained, holey, stinky rejects—end of story. As to the first pile, call your lucky friends and tell them to get their rear ends over to your house, *stat*. For great ways to dispose of the second and third, look to local chapters of organizations like Dress for Success, Salvation Army, and Goodwill.

The most important rule to follow here: Do not, under any circumstances, hang these items back in your closet! Get them out of your house as soon as possible, and experience a second wave of weightlessness as they exit the premises. Bye-bye!

Nothing is communicated so loudly as confidence. If you dress for your age with conviction, and without apologies, you stand the best possible chance at inhabiting your current life stage with grace, glamour, and panache. Aging isn't all about an accumulation of negatives—in fact, it opens up new opportunities that *aren't* available to that woman in her twenties. She may be able to rock the bohemian look in a way that could read as shabby on you, but you can wear the drama and elegance that might look like dress-up on her.

The Proper Care and Feeding of a Closet

So far, we've dealt mostly with what's *in* your closet—and what's definitely *out*. But the way your closet is kept, its organization or lack thereof, can be equally revealing. Its state can clue us in to how you *feel* about the way you look, and the things you own. A giant mess is essentially a blind spot or a black hole, the physical embodiment of an area of our lives we have decided to overlook. Does this describe your closet, and hence your approach to style?

I'm not suggesting that a functional closet needs to be pristine. But I do think that a healthy closet should act like a toolbox—everything in its place, ready to serve its specific function.

I like to see closets organized first by category and then by color, so that all of the dresses are hung together, in a rainbow of hues progressing from dark to light. Ditto for pants, blouses, and folded-up sweaters and tees. Our response to color being so emotional, this strategy offers a shortcut to dressing for our moods—whether we're grabbing for a cheerful orange tee because we're full of energy or because we're trying to perk ourselves up on a grayer day (an approach I cannot recommend enough). A closet organized by color and category also looks orderly, which is incredibly important on both a practical and an emotional level. Chaos breeds impulsive, thoughtless behavior—and it also makes it really hard to find things!

How will you ensure that your closet doesn't slip back into its old ways? I definitely don't believe in that old one-in, one-out rule, but here's the deal: If you hang on to clothes that are beginning to look old . . . you will soon be wearing old-looking clothes! So twice a year, when you're switching out your seasons, take an inventory of the clothing you're putting away. Check armpits for visible perspiration stains. Try an intensive course of laundering (a soak in hot water and OxiClean can work wonders, depending on the fabric); if that doesn't pan out, say good-bye. Look for holes—can they be repaired? Keep an eye out for general wear and tear—have the colors faded, is the fabric pilling? Though it can be more acceptable to wear worn-in clothes on the weekends, beware of your inner hoarder's not-so-hidden agenda. When she whispers, "Can't we just keep that for kicking around on the weekend?" take a moment to reflect on the consequences. Is "faded" really the statement you want to be making?

the compact of truth

what your closet reveals about you

You've taken the brave step of editing your wardrobe down to its leanest, meanest, sharpest self, which means it is now time to reflect on what you've learned. So much of this book is about looking and learning to *see*—so what did you see in there? What is your closet telling you? Focus your soul searching with the following prompts:

- Be *aware* of your addictions. I have never seen a closet that didn't reveal a plenitude of one particular type of garment, and a deficit in several other areas. Remember Anna's turtlenecks? Ugh, I will never understand women's love for turtlenecks—I mean, what does *that* say? To me, they're a classic example of clothing women wear when they want to hide, which is *exactly* the opposite of what I want for you. So what is abundant in your closet? Cardigans, dresses, sweaters? Clothing in the wrong colors or sizes? Take note of your pre-dilections for a certain type of clothing and ask yourself why it appeals.

- *Beware* of your camouflage. Ask yourself where your particular addiction comes from. Are you hoarding short skirts because you have legs up to your ears? Good for you—you're highlighting an asset (though we may need to have a chat about appropriateness). Are you stockpiling mannish, oversize button-down shirts because you want to hide your midsection? Not so good, though perfectly understandable. Turn back to page 131 to review my rules on using structured garments to cinch in the waist, and then repeat after me: Fitted Blazer. Fitted Blazer. Fitted Blazer. Are you hypnotized yet? Are you wearing a fitted blazer?

- Check your palette. What is the reigning color palette of your closet? Is it the one you should be living in? I often see blondes who are unconsciously drawn to brunette palettes, and vice versa, which is just such a travesty. Going through your closet will make it very, very easy to see where your color allegiances lie—and thus to experience a staggering transformation via a simple tweak to your palette. If you've been living in the wrong colors your entire life, prepare to be stunned. Color is *that* important—there's just no overstating it. Beyond the appropriateness of your chosen palette to your physical self, what does that palette say to the world? Are you hiding in a sea of drab? Where is the cheer in your closet? Where is the power?

▪ Perform a quality assurance check. Is your closet filled with crap? Again, I'm a huge fan of the low-budget find, but I do believe that every wardrobe should contain a certain number of high-quality investment pieces, particularly those I specified in Chapter 3. Consider what it is that prevents you from spending money on your clothing. Are you afraid of getting it wrong? Good thing I'm here to help! Not sure it's worthwhile or necessary? Reread Chapter 1. There is no underestimating the effect that your outward appearance can have on your life. *Our clothing has the power to help us manifest the goals, dreams, and desires we hold closest to our hearts.* Knowing this, how can you justify treating your wardrobe as if it doesn't matter?

- Read into the gaps. Have you gone through seventeen monsoon seasons without a good-looking raincoat or trench? Do you lack a single weekend outfit you feel good in? I'm going to chalk up these omissions to more than just forgetfulness or busyness. Ask yourself this: What in your belief system allows you to operate without these basic wardrobe necessities? This can be easier to suss out in a less emotional environment like, say, a kitchen—you wouldn't go three years without a colander or a pot big enough to boil water, would you? But we tend to bind up our identities in our clothes, so that instead of realizing we have a simple problem with a simple fix (the reason we can't ever figure out what to wear to work is that we are lacking a simple black or gray pencil skirt and a couple of good pairs of dark pants), we think of it as some kind of insurmountable emotional problem or an innate character flaw—"I'm just not a person who's ever dressed well at the office." Would you ever say that about your kitchen? "I'm just not a person who can keep a cutting board, a salad spinner, a good chef's knife in the house." See how absurd that sounds?

Think of this as an information-gathering session. What is standing in your way and preventing you from putting your best self forward, every day and in every way? Your closet will tell you—if you'll just listen.

Your Style Road Map

Whip out your trusty notebook, because we're going to take everything you've learned about yourself, in this chapter and throughout this process, and boil it down into a road map for your personal style.

STEP 1: IDENTIFY YOUR TOP THREE STYLE PRIORITIES. Go big here—we'll be working on that to-do list you've started in the next chapter, but here we are going for broader personal mantras. Maybe your priority is finding work clothes that are age-appropriate, or bringing a sense of play and flirtation into your closet. Anytime you're shopping or getting dressed and you feel yourself getting lost, you'll be able to return to these priorities and ask yourself whether what you are wearing brings you closer to or further away from fulfilling them.

STEP 2: IDENTIFY YOUR TOP THREE STYLE CHALLENGES. These challenges can be as specific as "finding work pants that don't gap at the waist" or "finding weekend clothes that are comfortable yet still flatter me." Committing your challenges to paper will encourage you to confront them rather than sweep them under the rug. Keep these challenges in mind as you're shopping, so that when you run into a piece of clothing that solves one of your challenges, you'll know to snag it right away.

chapter 6

a fresh new start
time to shop!

A respectable appearance is sufficient to make people more interested in your soul.
—*Karl Lagerfeld*

I hope you aren't yet sick of hanging out with your dear friend Rent-a-George, because the two of you are about to spend loads more time together. We've come to the moment you've undoubtedly been waiting for, the moment when we take everything we've learned in this book and get out and hit the stores.

After all of the hard labor we did in the last chapter, this next phase should be tons of fun. If I've learned anything from my years of helping clients sort out their style issues, it's that women, by and large, love to shop. Though they may be flummoxed by shopping, and often disappointed afterward, they do get carried away by the winds of fantasy those stores seem to promise—the lure of the fresh new thing that's bound to be transformative, the romance of a gorgeous silk dress.

Romance without rigor is what produces those bewildering closets you've heard so much about. Now that you have a backbone of style education and intention propping you up, you're going to be able to take those whims and turn them into the solid style decisions that will transform a series of confusing messages into a powerfully streamlined point of view. Let's get ready to shop . . .

Your Fashion To-Do List

This is no haphazard mission—you're going to be setting off on what is likely to be some of the most targeted, efficient, and rewarding shopping you've ever done in your life. Which is why before you hit the streets, we're going to take a few moments to get your fashion to-do list in order.

Look back at the notes you took during your closet purge, and add those items to the checklist you built in

Chapter 3. Then take this list and prioritize it, looking back at the top three fashion priorities you identified on page 211. Where do you most feel the gaps in your wardrobe? Are you desperately lacking in work-appropriate bottoms or bras that fit correctly? Do you have a specific event coming up? We'll make these our first orders of business, while also staying open to serendipity; some of your best finds will be those spur-of-the-moment items you pick up because something drew you to try them on.

While you're organizing your list, add any items as they occur—"wide black belt to break up taupe dress" or "opaque tights in a variety of colors."

Your Mission Statement

Here's where you pull it all together into the single, powerful statement of intention that will guide your expeditions; where all of the self-assessment you've been doing throughout this book should crystallize into a single moment of awareness. What is your dream? What led you to pick up this book? Your mission statement should remind you of that original intention, desire, hope, or wish, and connect it to the clothing you seek to acquire.

What is it that you seek, and how can your wardrobe help you get there? Hone all of your style wants into a short, catchy mission statement in the following mold: "I've been underselling myself in my career, and I'm through with that—I'm in the market for a wardrobe that will help me take my professional game to the next level." "I'm done hiding—I'm ready for clothes that tell the world to notice me." "I want to learn to love my body as it is today. I'm looking for pieces that fit me correctly and make no apologies about who I am." "I am looking for outfits that feel age-appropriate *and* exciting." "I am in the market for a wardrobe that feels more feminine and soft." "I am seeking outfits that exude confidence and power." "I am looking for the clothing that will help me attract a life partner." "I am in search of the clothing that will help me land my dream job."

What will your mission statement sound like? It all depends on where you are and what you are looking to accomplish. Whenever you are at a loss, you will be able to look back at this statement and assess whether the particular piece with which you are confronted gets you closer or further away from your big-picture goal.

Your Fashion Don'ts

Based on what you've learned so far and on what you saw in your closet, we're now going to create a do-not-pull list. This is essentially a punch list of your weaknesses, a catalog of those particular garments you don as safety blankets. This is the clothing you buy and reach for when you're on automatic pilot, the clothing that communicates nothing much, that camouflages you rather than drawing attention to you—in other words, it's the dead opposite of what you should be going for in your new, hyperconscious mode. Because you are inexplicably drawn to this clothing by forces greater than yourself, you're going to have to make a conscious effort *not* to accidentally veer toward it. Make a definitive "no turtlenecks, no khakis, no long-sleeved white tees" rule (insert your particular weaknesses here), and have George be on the lookout for any signs of regressive behavior. Eventually, these old friends will be nothing but distant memories—but for a while, you're going to have to use a little elbow grease in order to thwart their sinister hold.

Your Fashion Dares

Pledge to try on a few of the things that make you uncomfortable. Oftentimes, these are the pieces that highlight assets you may not have revealed in the past, or that stretch your conception of your style identity. They might be more formfitting or sexier than what you're used to, or more powerful than what you're used to, or more colorful than what you're used to, or in an entirely different style or size than you're used to. Or maybe they're all of those things.

What kinds of fears do these items bring up? This is the time to kick those qualms and doubts to the curb and try out a new, more confident identity. Maybe your particular pledge is to buy a skirt that hits you at mid-thigh—and to wear that skirt sometime within the next two weeks. You may well feel uncertain when you try that skirt on—and indeed, when you first wear it out. But give it a whirl. If it fits you correctly, flatters you, is in the right color palette, feels age-appropriate, and emits the right messages, odds are that once you're out the door you're going to be raking in compliments like never before. And trust me: *That* will get you feeling comfortable in no time.

Your Budget

Before you set out on your mission, you'll want to ballpark your overall budget. The particular number will differ for everyone, depending on your personal circumstances and on how much stuff you need. But I'm a firm believer in the fact that you don't have to drop serious coin in order to look great—it's all about knowing what colors and styles suit you best. And the beauty of shopping with your newly educated aesthetic is that you are going to be able to walk into any store, at any price point, and know what you look good in.

Getting the most bang for your buck doesn't, however, necessarily mean going for bottom-dollar discounts with every piece you purchase—sometimes an educated splurge can wear so well over time that on a cost-per-wear scale, it costs less than the sale-rack item. Maybe it's a designer bag that makes that H&M dress look like a million bucks. Maybe it's that $150 pair of jeans that fits you so well as to be completely revolutionary. (Though if those Gap or Old Navy jeans fit you like a dream, go for it and save your money for a beautiful silk blouse.)

If you want to look more powerful, you may have to spend some money in order to do that—but if that Theory or Calvin Klein suit is going to help you land that promotion or that new tony job, the money you spend is an investment that's only going to grow. Sometimes you have to spend money to make money.

So choose the places where you want to spend, whether we're talking about clothing, accessories, shoes, or makeup. You may find that Maybelline mascara does the job just great—but that you're willing to drop a little bit more money on the velvety lipstick you're going to be reapplying throughout the day.

If you fall in love with a piece whose price is causing you to break out in hives and that's going to have you scrimping for the next three months, don't do it. Everything in this book is about cultivating your consciousness, and we're not going to throw that all out the window when it comes to your wallet.

Where and How to Shop

For your first targeted excursion, select two to three stores to visit. One should be a department store—for my money, that's one of the best places for one-stop shopping, as it allows you to canvass a diverse array of brands and take care of your footwear, makeup, accessories, and lingerie needs while you're at it. A department store can also act as your fashion laboratory, offering a great opportunity for you to find out what brands you like and look good in, especially when it comes to highly fit-sensitive items like suiting and jeans. So within your budget, pick the department store with the best customer service, and if possible, go during an off time when it won't be too crowded or hectic.

Select one or two additional stores that cater to the kind of items you're looking for: affordable but great-looking work clothes, high-quality basics, interesting statement pieces, a great selection of footwear. Every town has a wonderful little boutique where you'll be able to find those one-of-a-kind items that you'll treasure for years to come. I always like to throw in one of those magical palaces of super-inexpensive retail as well if time allows—best to hit that as your last stop so you don't go into a discount clothing trance and blow your entire budget on what should be fun filler items.

Beware of your retail safety blankets. We all have them—those stores where we just feel comfortable. The price is right, we're comfortable with the fit, and we know we can always walk out with something passable. If you followed my instructions, you probably got rid of one or more bags of safe, unexciting, and vaguely unflattering clothing from this very store.

For one of my clients, it was an outdoor retailer with a line of ready-to-wear. Her closet was basically an advertisement for the brand, full of stuff I wasn't aware you could find next to a pair of hiking boots and a sleeping bag—dress pants and suits and dresses and all kinds of unflattering jeans. The explanation was that there was a flagship store near her home, and so it was just easy. She had a well-practiced formula for shopping there—she knew the layout, knew her sizes, and could just keep buying new versions of the same standards every time she walked in.

This kind of convenience shopping falls into the category of unconscious acquisition. It's our safety zone, the source of the multitude of 6s or 7s with which we fill our closets. Well, we want to do better than that. There's nothing wrong with basics or with having a uniform—so long as those basics and that uniform are treating you right. I'm not going to outlaw the occasional trip down memory lane, but a visit to this store should not be the first stop on your list. When you do return with all of our new standards fixed firmly in place, your experience should be quite different—you may find that your old favorite doesn't yield quite the bounty it used to. Or, on the contrary, you may find a few unexpectedly great surprises lurking in corners you wouldn't have visited before.

Carve Out a Relationship

Even though you'll have your trusty Rent-a-George by your side, you'll still want to avail yourself of the services of a knowledgeable salesperson if you can. Though it can be easier to slide under the radar at giant department stores and large chains (as opposed to small boutiques where you're bound to be looked after), asking for help is still worthwhile. Salespeople work for commissions—so it's in their best interest to give you the service that gets you out the door with a smile on your face and a bulging bag full of great goodies. Don't assume that they're just trying to get you to buy, buy, buy—they want a happy return customer just as much as they want the sale, so it's *not* in their interest to have you coming back with a whole bunch of stuff you're not pleased with the next day.

Look for a friendly face and let that person know what you're searching for. Tell them about your usual struggles regarding fit, and give them information about the colors you're interested in. They should be more than happy to steer you in the right direction, make suggestions about particular pieces or brands that might work well for your body type, and pull the sizes you need.

Particularly in those large, disorienting department stores, don't get caught in the trap of wandering around aimlessly. Ask questions—where are the jeans, how do I find the lingerie department? Wandering can be a decent way to shop when you're browsing, but when you're on a targeted mission you want to maximize your time.

If you're in an environment where help is not forthcoming, make the most of your George. Have him work for that free lunch he has more than earned. If you need sizes and there's no one around to pull them for you, he's your man. I want you focusing on the all-important task of trying on and assessing these pieces. Divide and conquer, and let him exercise his judgment, too. Be open to his suggestions and opinions—an impartial set of eyes is an invaluable tool.

Knowing What to Pull

Pulling the right clothes is an art as much as it is a science. There are going to be mistakes—that's why we try things on before buying them—but you can maximize your odds of dressing room success by heeding the following tips:

LET COLOR BE YOUR GUIDE. Your color palette is your most effective compass, helping to steer you quickly and efficiently through that maze of racks and cutting out a huge range of off-color time-wasters that are guaranteed *not* to flatter. So let the color wheel be your guide. Scan the floor for items in your palette, pull anything that interests you, and grab a few wild cards as well.

THINK IN OUTFITS. Don't just pull a pair of pants—pull a top or two to go with those pants, and a jacket to throw on over the outfit. (And grab a high-heeled shoe and a flat to try on with everything while you're at it.) If you find a great brand that's really working for you, don't be afraid to pull outfits within that brand. These pieces are guaranteed to work well together because they speak in the same aesthetic idiom, are cut from the same cloth, and were pigmented by the same dye lots—all of which is going to make it a lot easier to get at the harmony we've been talking about.

SEEK OUT LUXURIOUS FABRICS. Whether we're talking about basics or more dressed-up pieces, great fabric can mean the difference between ho-hum and fabulous. In fact, you may be able to make some of the upgrades you're after in your wardrobe just by switching up the fabric in a familiar seeming piece. In a tee, fabric means the difference between flattering and boxy; in a button-down, between business-as-usual and glam-squad career woman. Fabric can spell the difference between a basic that's totally forgettable and a signature piece you can't live without—so go for those softer-than-soft silks, those lush cashmeres, those luxurious wools, those expensive-feeling linens. Don't just use your eyes—reach out and touch.

SUSPEND YOUR JUDGMENT. It can be very difficult to tell from the hanger how something is actually going to fit, so suspend your judgment until you've tried something on. An item that looks like a total rag on the floor can fit beautifully, and vice versa. Drape rarely looks good on the hanger, but it can look amazing on you. Try stuff on for curiosity's sake—if an item is in your colors and looks interesting but strange, and you cannot for the life of you tell what it's going to look like, give it a whirl. You never know.

REMEMBER YOUR SHAPES. Hold things up to assess their overall shape. Fit can be hard to divine until you're in the dressing room, but some things are obvious. (Does it have a waist? Is it fitted in the right places?) If a piece is loaded with fit features that have been problematic for you in the past, don't bother.

LOOK FOR INTEREST. Every piece that you pull should have *something* going for it. Especially when it comes to clothing that falls outside the pantheon of cherished classics (pencil skirts, shift dresses, suiting), you want it to have some quality that makes it stand out. What makes this piece interesting and unique? It could be the subtlest detail or texture or the boldest of patterns—interest doesn't always have to scream for attention.

PULL CLOTHES IN QUANTITY. When my clients and I exit the dressing room, the cleanup is inevitably epic—but the salespeople never mind, because we're giving them great business (as well as free entertainment). As you make your way through the store, know your goals, but don't be shy about trying on a ton of stuff. To get at that most excellent fit you now require, you're going to have to kiss a lot more frogs—but you'll wind up finding a lot more princes, too.

Dressing Room Smarts

When it comes time to step inside that dressing room, it's all about what happens in the mirror. So take your time in there, and pay attention to how you feel and to how your posture is affected by what you have on. Does that jacket make you stand up straight and assume a power position, or have you shrinking like a wallflower? What does it say, and how does it make you feel? Above all, remember that you're going after a new standard now, the golden rule of the perfect 10. Be ruthless in your judgments, and trust your instincts.

When a Garment Calls Your Name

Whether you're on a targeted shopping mission or you just wandered into a boutique on a balmy Sunday afternoon, if you see a piece of clothing that screams your name—and that seems like it might possess all of the essential qualities described on page 102—stop and try it on. Because sometimes, these garments that really jump out at us can be more than perfect 10s, pieces that are so ineffably right they just seem to capture the essence of our personalities. For one of my clients, it was a flowy, belted black silk dress with a bright floral pattern we picked up at a little store in Manhattan's West Village. It had a vintage feeling, a kind of dark drama, and was sexy and modest all at once, with a whiff of the Italian countryside about it. It became her favorite dress, and the item of clothing she got the most compliments on.

Snap those pieces up when you find them, regardless of whether they're what you're looking for at that particular moment. Odds are you won't regret it.

FOR SEPARATES, TRY TO GO BY THE RULE OF THREE. Come up with two to three ways to wear the item. Can that tunic be cinched in with a belt over jeans and flats, worn with leggings or fitted pants and a heel, and maybe even paired with dark tights and boots for the winter? Sounds like a winner. Can that tee be tucked into an A-line skirt with espadrilles as well as tossed over jeans? Worn under a blazer? You get the picture.

MAKE SURE THOSE PRICIER PIECES WILL EARN THEIR KEEP. What else can you wear with those pants? If you're on the fence about a more expensive item, ask the salesperson to help you find other pieces to pair with it. If you're in an expensive store, you don't have to buy those exact items; they might spark an idea for items you may get more cheaply elsewhere in order to make that piece multitask.

WALK THE RUNWAY FOR YOUR RENT-A-GEORGE. Come on out and show George everything that has a fighting chance. As I've said, an extra set of eyes is an invaluable tool. But there's also the fact that making a whole bunch of decisions on your own can be exhausting—sharing the burden with another person takes a whole lot of weight off you.

CONSIDER HOW AN ITEM FITS INTO YOUR WARDROBE. Does it immediately bring to mind a few compatible pieces you already own? Require a specific piece you'd be happy to acquire? If neither of those things is true, walk away. Don't buy a piece you have no idea how to wear and figure you'll get around to making work someday—it's likely to sit in your closet unworn for years.

DON'T OVERDUPLICATE. As I've said, especially when it comes to basics like that navy cardigan or those go-with-everything taupe flats, having duplicates (or near duplicates) of an item is essential. But you don't want to get caught in the pattern of just buying the same things over and over again. So if you fall in love with a familiar seeming black tunic, ask yourself whether you already have its equivalent.

CHECK FOR FIT PERFECTION. Before you set out on your mission, review the rules of fit and proportion on pages 57 to 62—obviously, you'll be checking every item you try on to make sure that it fits you like a glove. But if you fall in love with something that doesn't feel quite right in the fit department, check in with Rent-a-George to see whether you both agree that it's a situation a tailor can handle. Pants that are too long or that gap in the waist and fitted blazers that don't quite skim the ribs are two common candidates for alterations.

SNAG IT. If an item is a no-holds-barred, no-doubt-about-it 10 that has both you and George transfixed by your reflection—whether said item appears on your checklist or not—don't hem and haw. Read the tea leaves. If the universe is telling you to buy that bold red dress with the silver accents (even though you aren't exactly sure where you're going to wear it), heed its all-knowing message!

Zen and the Art of Shopping

Stores can be overwhelming, sending women into a frantic state of mind that's ground zero for the style mistakes that bedevil their wardrobes; or into a spiral of self-criticism that has them nixing possibilities without ever giving them a chance. When it comes to shopping, panic and self-doubt are your mortal enemies—I can't tell you how many clients have explained away mistakes by telling me that they were having a miserable shopping day and just wanted to get it over with.

First of all, remain calm. You are a shopping ninja.

You are not being judged by these clothes—you are judging them. You are the sole arbiter of fit and taste in this scenario—not the clothes or the designers who made them.

When you try on a piece that doesn't work for you, don't despair. In an ideal world, we'd all be wearing only bespoke clothing that was tailored just for us. But that's not the world we live in. Given how many shapes and sizes the human body can come in, it stands to reason that mass-manufactured clothing is going to fit some people and not others. When something doesn't fit, simply place it in the "No" pile and move on. If, however, you're in a store where you're finding that little to nothing is fitting, head for the hills—that store isn't for you. (Conversely, if you find a boutique where everything fits you like a dream, don't be shy about loading up on stuff—and yes, please do come again!)

Dress comfortably, stay hydrated, and never shop hungry. Eat a healthy breakfast, and bring a snack if you need to. Think of a shopping expedition like the SATs—it's a high-octane mission to which you want to bring your A-game. Yes, it can be exhausting. You're covering a lot of ground, making a lot of decisions, and basically doing sets of burpees in that dressing room. So breathe, and keep your eye on the prize. The mind-set from which you approach your shopping expedition will have significant ramifications on its outcome.

The Trend Question

Most of the women I work with are not followers of trends. In fact, my clients tend to fear trends, looking upon them as a form of Martian code they'd need an inter-galactic interpreter to understand. If that describes you, you can pat yourself on the back—your trendlessness has just earned the blessing of George B Style. Because trends come and go, it is far more important to know what you look good in, to understand your colors, your silhouettes, and the message you want to get across, than to know what's "on trend" at any given moment.

Will you look dated if you disregard the trends? Not at all. These days, the stores are so saturated with trends that you'd have a hard time avoiding them even if you wanted to. And we don't necessarily want you to. On the contrary, we want you to look current—but we want you to get there by starting with a classic foundation and then experimenting with those trends that work for your body, your coloring, and your age. *Work* is the key word here— *the trend must work for you.* If your legs aren't your greatest assets and you're seeing short skirts everywhere you turn, you do *not* need to run with that trend. If neon green is sweeping the nation and you're anyone but a dark-skinned brunette, steer clear unless you enjoy looking tubercular—or try touches of the color in your accessories if you must.

Shopping Online and Hitting the Sales

As you can probably guess, I am not a huge proponent of online shopping. I know it's convenient, and that many women buy clothes online and are fully capable of returning them if they don't fit correctly—but I also know that many of you make online purchases that don't work out and then never return them, because it's too much of a pain. This is how you accumulate a closetful of mistakes.

There *are,* however, some things that can be safely purchased online: accessories, makeup, jewelry, shoes (particularly if you know the brand and are willing to make returns), and those basics you're rebuying because they've worn out. If you're *very* comfortable with a brand and know that their pants always fit you, I'll make another exception there.

Sales are another matter altogether. While in the past, you may have thought of the sale as a land-mine-strewn disaster zone from which you were unlikely to exit unscathed (the inevitable nonreturnable mistake in tow), your whole experience is about to be transformed. In fact, you will be most in love with this book when it comes time to hit those sales—because you will now be approaching them with a strong and confident point of view that is going to net you a much higher proportion of successes.

Before you hit a sale, do a quick closet inventory and identify what you need—sale time is a great time to replace things. Above all, remain calm. Do not lower your standards because an item is on sale! Even an item that costs fifteen dollars will take up space in your closet, so you always have to ask yourself whether it's worthy of a spot in your sacred space. Maybe that fifteen dollars should be put toward that full-price leather jacket you've had your eye on. (Obviously, if it's great, go for it.)

Look out for styling imperfections. Some items are marked down because of subtle manufacturing flaws.

That can be just fine if the flaws really are subtle—but sometimes you'll get home and realize that the pattern on your new shirt is totally crooked, and you just can't wear it because it's going to drive you crazy.

Speaking of crazy: Steer clear of the crazy-cakes sale purchase. Sale time *can* be a great time to experiment with new, more out-there looks you wouldn't be comfortable shelling out the full-price dollars for. But make sure that the item really does stand a chance at being worn.

Beware of the lure of false math. Those "You just saved $347!" receipts are especially tricky and extremely effective at making us feel like we've basically won the lottery. But let's face it: You didn't really just save $347—you spent $250. So look at the total price rather than paying too much attention to the discount, and be honest with yourself about how much you can or should spend. Know that when it comes to clothing, retail pricing is all about perceived value. Even at a vast markdown, the designer and retailer are still likely to be making a sizable profit—so don't fool yourself into thinking you're getting the items at cost.

Your Look Book

No rest for the weary. Once you've hauled home your loot, the real work begins. Instead of just stashing the stuff away and hoping it sprinkles its magical fairy dust over your life, you're going to move on to the next order of business: building the Look Book that's going to help you figure out how to wear all of this new loot.

Many of you won't actually need a physical Look Book—the term can be loosely interpreted to suggest the mental catalog you're going to be collecting. But I know from experience that some of you *do* need a true Look Book. If you've always struggled with style, with knowing how to put together an outfit, if you downright hate even thinking about this stuff, such a catalog might be the thing that changes your life. I've had clients who couldn't do without them. Megan, of the full-blown outdoor-retail addiction, was one. Once we'd stocked her closet with several months' worth of shopping trips and prepped her with multiple styling sessions, she was looking terrific and feeling it, too. But a few months later, I got one of those frantic calls: "I just can't figure it out—I know we got me tons of stuff but I still feel like I have nothing to wear!"

She had plenty to wear, of course, but because she wasn't a clothes-minded person to begin with, she'd been unable to remember the looks we created and couldn't figure out how to pull it all together. Girl needed a Look Book, simple as that. So we restyled her closet, showing her two to three ways to wear every item and styling her down to the shoes, jewelry, and outerwear—and this time I took tons of pictures.

If you feel like you don't need a visual Look Book but could use some help for those uninspired mornings when you're looking at your closet and drawing a blank, you may just want to take a few notes on what pairs well with what.

So take each of the new items you've purchased and style them to the nines (or rather, to the 10s). Find the things you already own that pair well with the new stuff. Take that suit and deconstruct it. Can the pants be paired with a light, slouchy crewneck sweater and flats for an everyday office look? Can the blazer be worn over jeans and a T-shirt? Take a picture. Try taking it to a night look as well, throwing that blazer over fitted pants and your slinkiest special-occasion tank. Don't stop at the clothes—try on a few pairs of shoes and your jewelry as well. I often find that an outfit just isn't coming together until we have the right necklace on—and that the choice of necklace is likely to affect the choice of shoe.

Be adventurous. You never know until you have it on. It may sound crazy to pair that zigzag-patterned top with a polka-dotted bubble skirt and a pair of strappy orange platforms, but this is an outfit I recently put on one of my clients—and lo and behold, it looked *fierce*. Have fun with it. Be inspired, and work with those themes. Is there a touch of the flapper in that floaty little black dress you just picked up? Then try it out with loads of pearls, some red heels, an ultradark eye, and your most devilish lipstick. Use your imagination, and you'll be rewarded with tons of new surprises. A new item may give an unexpected lift to a nearly forgotten hand-me-down, which could all of a sudden become your new favorite piece.

Whether you have Rent-a-George snap photos of each and every outfit and painstakingly create a personal online Look Book using a site like Pinterest or an app like Stylebook (printing out the photos and pasting them into a scrapbook is also an option) or just choose to take some notes on a few unexpected combinations, this process is going to make the difference between mornings spent in confusion and a seamless dressing routine that is perfectly cued to your mood and to what the day holds. You'll be able to grab that houndstooth pencil skirt and instantly know which three options you can choose to pair with it.

A styling clinic is a great thing to do with all the items in your closet—not just the new stuff you're hauling in.

Think of it as a rainy-day alternative to house cleaning. In my book, styling your closet *does* count as doing your chores (even though it's all fun and no drudgery).

Your Transitional Wardrobe

It's all well and good to consider a calm and conscious shopping expedition under the very best circumstances. But I know that there are times when we are confronted by radically different, new realities that pitch us into full-frontal wardrobe crises.

Motherhood, for example, is a life stage through which I've guided many a client. I worked with Amy, an interior decorator, through her single days, through the launch of her business, and through her engagement and marriage. Now she's a new mom to an eight-week-old baby, calling me in an absolute panic because she can't fit into anything in her closet, she's got two hours between client appointments and showroom visits, and she needs me to please, please, *please* meet her on the corner of Charles and Bleecker and take her shopping because she cannot spend another day in the same beaten-down pair of pants.

The clothing she needs for this life stage, with its hallmark sleep deprivation, weight fluctuations, and proximity to volatile bodily fluids, can't be the same kind we got for her when she was single or first married—the structured pants and pencil skirts in dry-clean-only fabrics, the translucent silk blouses and long, delicate necklaces. But it still has to be clothing that represents her as a working professional, and as an individual whose identity is composed of more than her diaper bag and her cherub-cheeked infant. The fix: We loaded her up with several pairs of terrific jeans in various washes and colors, and armfuls of soft, silky dress tees in a variety of styles (boatneck, V-neck, short-sleeve, long-sleeve). A few long, drapey sweaters and colorful ballerina flats later, she was feeling and looking great.

Now, instead of unfavorably comparing herself to all the other moms on the playground—and New York City playgrounds can be *intense*—Amy had a look she could feel confident about. No matter what her changing load of priorities and obligations amounted to, it was still important to her that she look presentable, and beyond that, stylish and cute. I've heard enough new moms wail about their wardrobe's failings to know that she isn't alone in this, and to understand how challenging these transitional periods can be.

When we fall apart at the seams in the face of any kind of dramatic change—whether it's rapid weight loss or gain or a sudden job change—discomfort rules our days. That's why it's so important to check in with your wardrobe whenever you're going through such a transition, to see whether it still fits both your body and your life—and, most important, that it still expresses the message you want to be putting out there.

If you know this phase is only going to be temporary, hold on to your old clothes—and hit those budget stores to find the deals.

Building Your Wardrobe over Time

These targeted shopping missions geared toward filling specific gaps in your closet are a giant step forward. But odds are that you aren't going to be able to fully refurbish your wardrobe within a month, or two months, or even three. Why? Because there's an element of serendipity at work in finding those perfect 10s. Because styles are seasonal, so at minimum you'll have to tackle the process over the course of a year. Because our lives and our bodies and our circumstances change over time, our wardrobe must evolve along with them. And also because most of us simply can't afford to spend so much money all in one go, or withstand that much decision making in such a concentrated period of time.

This is a good thing. By building your wardrobe over time, rather than gunning for an overnight transformation like those depicted by the denizens of *la télé-réalité*, you'll be honing your eye and educating your aesthetic as you go. Shop as consciously as you dress, and take your time.

chapter 7

a fresh new start for him
a mini guide to making over your man

All it takes are a few simple outfits. And there's one secret: the simpler the better.
—Cary Grant

Dress up your sportswear and dress down your formalwear.
—Luciano Barbera

We hereby interrupt our programming to bring you a special public service announcement. This message pertains to a grave fashion emergency, a blasphemy against the laws of style that is likely to be occurring right under your nose. While the rest of this book concerns a personal journey, in this chapter we will be making room for a little bit of altruistic action on the part of a person you know and love, a person in desperate need of your help: your man.

How do men err when it comes to fashion? Let me count the ways. I'm asked to intervene in this arena so frequently that I should start considering a package deal—make over your man for just $49.95 extra! And it's not just the wives and girlfriends asking me to make over their men—the guys often sidle up to me when they think she's not listening to ask if I can help them out, too. Odds are that once he witnesses your transformation, he's going to be angling to get some of that newfound mojo for himself.

While you may have tried similar stunts in the past with limited or partial success, I'm sure you're eager to know how to use your newfound command of style to enact a more effective transformation on your man. Read on, but please note that there are certain situations in which subterfuge and/or manipulation may be called for. I'm confident you'll be up to the task.

It's All About the Fit . . .

Nothing spells schlub like a pair of oversize, faded, fifteen-year-old jeans and a big baggy tee or polo shirt. And it saddens me to say that this is *such* a common sight. The absolute number-one style offense I see in menswear is guys wearing their clothes way too big. I'm not just talking about a preference for a boxier suit here—I'm talking about men simply wearing their clothing in the wrong sizes. The pant, the blazer, the shirt, the shorts, you name it. And just as with women's clothes, men's clothes are going to look their best when they fit correctly, allowing us to see the silhouette of his body.

This can be a tough one to tackle, because though the fix is as simple as can be, the problem's root cause is psychological: Men fear that if their clothes are too tight, they won't look masculine. Memo to the world: Caring about how you look and wearing clothes that fit does not make a man unmasculine—it makes him dapper and manly, as opposed to juvenile and messy! If your man is balking at the notion of going down a jean size (or two) because he's afraid his manliness will be impugned, it's time to pull out the *Mad Men* or 007 slideshow. Talk about tailored clothes that fit to the nines! (And if Don Draper and James Bond aren't masculine, then I don't know who is.)

You do occasionally see men with the opposite problem, generally surrounding the gradual growth of their midsections and their lack of acceptance thereof. If your sweetie's beer belly is putting some undue strain and stress on those shirt buttons, it's time to either have him refitted or get him to the gym. I'll never forget the sight of one client in a super-chic five-thousand-dollar Tom Ford suit whose skin was peeking out between the buttons of his shirt . . . I still shudder when I think about that!

Getting the Details Right

Menswear may be infinitely simpler than women's clothing, with far less variety when it comes to shapes, styles, patterns, colors, and types of garments; but in the realm of men's suiting, there are a fairly dizzying number of *very* specific rules and details. The length and width of the tie, the length of the cuff, the presence or absence of the cuff link, whether a blazer should be worn open or closed, whether a collar should be buttoned down or left askew, the color of the sock, the color of the shoe, and on and on and on. Unless your man is actually interested in fashion, this is a department in which you're both going to need some help. So just as you did when you shopped for yourself, you're going to find a friendly salesperson and get them to help you style the suit.

Suiting conventions aside, it really all comes back to fit. It doesn't matter how nice the fabric is—if the suit is too big, it's going to look terrible, which is why getting men into the correct size is the absolute first thing I do. Just as with your clothes, his will look best when we can see the line of his body. Know that most suits will require some degree of alteration, whether it's getting the cuffs or pants shortened or taking the waist in; that's where a good tailor comes in, whether he's on site at the department store or has his own shop.

If your man has trouble fitting into off-the-rack suits because of his body shape, look into custom suiting. A lot of the newer custom lines aren't as expensive as bespoke suiting was in the past. And if that's the only way to get him the right fit, it's definitely going to be worth it.

The Importance of the Purge

Beyond the fit issue, one of the most common problems I see in men's closets is a *major* refusal to update. Men simply *hate* replacing their clothes. Many of them don't like thinking about clothing at all, never mind shopping for it. And so they hold on to their clothes until they are threadbare and far beyond repair. Why fix it unless it's broken, the thinking goes.

Hoarding and gross negligence are not uncommon. I had one client whose husband's extreme hoarding had banished her all the way to the coat closet; she offered me a bonus for convincing him to get rid of half of his stuff. (Naturally, I succeeded.)

Once, in a lawyer's closet, I was confronted with an unsavory situation in which nearly every other shirt and tie was stained with food. This had traveled beyond the usual wear and tear and into the category of epic slobbishness. Even after I called him out—and I was *not* using my indoor voice—he tried to plead his case, as any good lawyer would. "Suits are expensive, and those clothes still fit me." "Some of them are pretty new." "Anyway, I doubt anyone is looking closely enough to notice." It was my pleasure to inform him that in fact, people were noticing. The jury had deliberated and come back with a verdict of guilty as charged.

The good news is that because men's fashion is somewhat less complicated—the options being fewer—once you get the bad stuff out and get some good stuff in, it's going to be much easier to bring his closet up to speed.

So just as you did with your own wardrobe, before you hit the stores you're going to want to gently guide him through a closet purge of his own. You may not be able to persuade him to try everything on, but do attempt to pick up and assess every single piece, making a punch list of the items he needs. This process isn't likely to be nearly as emotional for him as it was for you—we simply don't put the same pressures on men's bodies, and as a result, their feelings toward their clothes aren't quite so complicated. But you may run into some resistance and emotional baggage when it comes to those T-shirts he's held on to since college, or even since high school. Guys can be sentimental, too!

Your Man on the Weekend

Power through that resistance, because finding an acceptable casual look for your man is key. This is the area where so many of the men fall down on the job and dress like overgrown teenagers. Free of their structured work uniforms, they tend to consider the weekend a holy bastion of "me time" in which the full brunt of their slovenly ways can be unleashed. This is when the beer-logo and band tees come out in force, along with the worst of the pleated khakis and the XXL shorts, jeans, and sweats. Isn't it relaxing? Isn't it romantic?

Pleated pants, in all of their myriad categories of offensiveness, are worthy of a chapter of their own, but I'll try to keep it brief: The pleated pant, most especially when it comes to casual wear, should be banished from this world altogether! At the least, it should be reserved for only the sveltest and most stylish of menfolk. While it can be pulled off to a sort of retro, Gatsby-ish effect, such a look requires a certain body type and a highly advanced style IQ. Trust me on this one. Flat-front and pleated trends may come and go, but for most men, the pleat is not going to be a flattering look.

Men often bring up comfort as a reason for their dedication to their oversize weekend duds. Again, this is where you may have to get him into the store, trying on pants that actually fit, before he sees the error of his ways. A pant that fits correctly should not be uncomfortable, though the whole ensemble *should* make him stand up a little straighter. Speaking of pants: Make sure you don't walk out of that store without at least one sexy pair of jeans that fit him just great. Feel free to objectify him in the dressing room to hammer your point home.

The Lure of Memorabilia

Tees, sweatshirts, and (gasp) jerseys represent another very common pain point in the masculine wardrobe, with sentimentality often playing a large part. In the same way that women hold on to their skinny clothes in an aspirational fantasy that does their closets way more harm than good, men hold on to their band and concert tees as a way of grasping on to youthful times past. The men just *love* to hoard that wearable memorabilia, whether it's music or sports or college related.

This may be an area where you need to do a pass through a store before you can make headway—once he sees how much better he looks in grown-up tees and cotton or cashmere crewnecks in the right size and in a bevy of the colors that flatter his palette, he may be ready to take another look at those oh-so-juvenile message tees and zip-up hoodies.

The struggle with sports-themed clothing may pose particular challenges of the over-my-dead-body variety, so you'll want to tread with care. You may start by proposing to limit the occasions to which the sports memorabilia is worn. An actual sports event is an example of a *good* place to wear that team jersey and cap. So is that Little League game. Brunch at your parents' or a meeting with your financial advisor? Not so much.

Men love nothing so much as weekend clothing that reminds them of their favorite leisure time activities—and so it is that the vacations spawn the Hawaiian shirts and the sporting events beget the dreaded jerseys, caps, tees, and sweats. The key to turning him around is finding casual styles that really do look like something he could wear on vacation, but for an upscale stay at a deluxe resort rather than a depressing week at the Motel 6. Think Bermuda shorts that actually fit him and cool linen shirts in a range of flattering colors. Again, when in doubt, let Don Draper be his guide.

What you want to do is upgrade his signature casual style. If he's a tracksuit kind of guy, see if you can get him into a better version of his standard, with a cute pair of sneakers and a few tees in flattering colors and better fabrics. Get him to stretch out of his comfort zone with a pair of fitted khakis and a great-looking gingham shirt. Or pair those new jeans with a fitted cashmere or cotton sweater, a diving watch, a pair of desert boots, and a casual blazer. If it's jeans and a tee, top your rock star off with a cool leather jacket.

The Pop of Color

It probably won't surprise you to hear that I'm *quite* comfortable in a cherry-red blazer. But I work in fashion, and not in finance. So I get that color can be a challenge for the guys, and I know that most often in menswear we see color restricted to the shirts and ties, and often to a fairly limited palette. If a guy is not into color or works in an environment where only blues and the occasional red tie can pass muster, it is *of course* okay for him to stick to the basics. A white button-down shirt under a dark suit can be a classic thing of beauty. But try nudging him to experiment with some color in his weekend wardrobe; this can be a great time for him to express himself.

Regardless of his work environment or his general attitude toward color, make a point of introducing him to the colors in which he will look best. Share the gift of color awareness by turning back to Chapter 4 and making note of the palette that will do right by his good looks. Be sure that, at the least, he owns several tees in the colors that pop his eyes and hair and brighten his complexion.

If he's open to it, go for the full color-oriented makeover. Fill his closet with the tees, sweaters, shirts, ties, and jackets that make him shine.

Dressing for the Occasion

Weddings. Cocktail parties. Christmas dinners. Celebratory brunches. These are the events that have confounded mankind since time immemorial. Dressing for the occasion tends not to be a strong suit among the menfolk, probably because it requires a bit of extra attention and forethought, neither of which they generally want to apply to their clothing. Most men dress in uniforms—one for work, one for the weekend. Any event that deviates from the standard is cause for consternation and befuddlement.

As you gradually begin to upgrade his wardrobe and fill out its obvious gaps and weak points, dressing for these events should become less challenging; for those particularly important social or work engagements like weddings or crucial job interviews, gently encourage him to think in advance about what he's going to wear, so there's time to do some shopping if necessary.

The Shoe Question

The shoes make the man, as they say, and they've been the unmaking of many a fellow as well. Let's face it: You are probably ready to throw out every pair he has—all two of them. Men have the worst taste in shoes. And whether it's a pair of hopelessly outdated, scuffed loafers (always in standard-issue black or brown) or a clunky pair of all-purpose sneakers, habits die hard in this realm.

Prepare to make a significant investment in diversifying his shoescape—and then to help him remember to switch out his shoes so he doesn't get stuck back in the same rut. When in doubt, go with a classic. A beautiful suede loafer looks great and simplifies things, especially when you're dealing with someone who doesn't want to put much thought into the matter. Make sure his closet includes a good-looking pair of sneakers, up-to-date loafers, boat shoes, boots, and some flip-flops you can stand to look at. Introduce some color into the mix—for spring and summer, a salmon or pale blue pair of dockers can really pop a pair of khakis and a crisp checkered button-down shirt.

While you're at it, go ahead and banish those wrap-around sunglasses and get him into a pair of stylish frames; like watches, great sunglasses can be the accessory that pulls together his look.

The Importance of Grooming

Oh, the comb-overs I've rescued. It's a difficult subject to broach, but broach it we must.

Listen. Men have a very hard time admitting that they're balding. It's a humbling rite of passage that brings up anxieties about aging, desirability, even virility. And many men would rather shut their eyes to the problem than tackle it head-on. Because there is no one else in his life who is going to hold his hand and help him through this fragile transition, it will probably fall to you to step up to the plate.

If you're getting into a situation where you're beginning to be able to see the top of his head shining through, it's time to gently take out the pictures of Matt Lauer, pre- and post-buzz cut. A shaved or buzzed or close-cropped head can be downright sexy. Thinning hair? Not so much. You never want to be known as the balding guy who's in denial—much better to be known as the guy with the confidently shaved head. Once again, it's all about embracing your current life stage and working with what you've got; hiding is just as ineffective for men as it is for women.

Once you've gotten past the initial crop, it's all about the upkeep. Depending on the length of the cut, you may want to pick up an electric razor so he can DIY; but many men with buzz cuts, particularly those that are very close-shaven, enjoy a good old-fashioned weekly or biweekly visit to the barber.

Especially when the hair is very short, keeping the facial hair neatly groomed becomes of the utmost importance—though this really goes for all men. Because we're not going to be putting makeup on him, the key transformation will generally have to do with taking his grooming habits up a notch. Get rid of that facial hair altogether, or take him to the barber to have that beard neatly trimmed. Give him a little polish. It goes without saying that, balding or not, he will very likely need to be taken by the hand and shown the way to a better haircut. His stylist should be just as talented as yours.

While we're on the subject of grooming: *Please, please, please* have pity on the rest of the world and take him to the nail salon to deal with those claws he's growing on his hands and feet! It's all about the details, and that fabulous shirt and tie combination will count for nothing if his colleagues catch sight of his dirt-encrusted talons.

Dressing for Presence

When the average Joe isn't committing a major fashion felony, he's generally guilty of the lower-impact crime of being a complete and utter fashion *snooze*. Because most men aren't thinking much about what their clothing is doing for them, they're largely focused on getting to a 6 on the scale of acceptability. Looking okay or acceptable or good enough (or even just clean!) pretty much sums up their ambitions. Which is why trying to convince an alpha male to add interest to his look is like conning a small child into eating a plate full of spinach.

If you're sick of seeing your honey stuck in the drabbest of getups, try talking to him about some of the ideas we discussed at the beginning of the book. The goal here is not to dress a man in a more interesting way so that he can ascend a rung of the ladder of haute couture—what we're talking about is using color, pattern, and texture to bolster his presence. Depending on the situation, that can translate to an easier time gaining command of a room, an increased ability to charm his way to the desired outcome in a meeting, and maybe even a more frictionless dinner at his in-laws'. Who wouldn't want that?

chapter 8

the new you
manifesting the change you seek

I'm going to be totally honest with you. This moment, when I send you off into the good night in your bright and shining new wardrobe, can be cathartic not only for you, but for me as well. Watching my clients go through the process of change is absolutely the most rewarding part of my work as a stylist. I get to be a witness to their stunned squeals of delight, their incredulous assessments of the results— *"I can't believe how much better this looks"* or (very commonly) *"What was I thinking??"*—and those breathless mid-event bathroom-stall phone calls giving me the rundown on all the fabulous compliments they received. But in this case—unless you tweet me your before-and-after pics, which I *highly* encourage you to do—I won't get to be right there with you. And I'm truly, truly sorry about that, because watching a person come into their own really is a gift.

As I have been telling you again and again throughout this book, while your closet is an ever-changing entity, never quite reaching a static state of perfection but always evolving through time, even the smallest tweaks you make to your wardrobe are going to have an immediate and life-altering effect. This stuff is powerful.

Gird yourself for attention and compliments, because you are about to receive sizable doses of both. When you dress to be seen, you should not be surprised that you *will* be seen. And the funny thing about friends, colleagues, and even the most distant of acquaintances is that they *love* giving compliments. They love noticing change, and letting you know that they've noticed—especially when they notice not just one great outfit here and there, but an overarching pattern of radical improvement. Behind their compliments lie a couple of questions: *What's your secret?* (They want to know, because they want to look just as great!) And: *What's the reason?*

When people shower you with compliments about your appearance, it is because they are assuming that something in your life must be going very, very right. They aren't just telling you they like your shirt or your new hairstyle. They're telling you that you look happier, more successful, and more self-assured. They've noticed, and they understand what a big deal it is.

Pay attention to those compliments. Because of the work you have been doing throughout this book, you are now ready to be the sole and most important judge of the statements your style is emitting—but a little bit of external feedback never hurts.

I'm pretty sure you wouldn't have picked up this book if you weren't looking for change. But even if you *think* you're ready for change, when it actually comes to pass you may be a bit surprised by how truly *different* things feel. Change can be difficult, no matter how ready we think we are for its siren call.

There may be some discomfort. As I said, you will be attracting more attention than you have in the past, which means that there may be an adjustment period where you get used to walking around in those new boots of yours. A client of mine recently shot me an email telling me she was suddenly getting honked at and catcalled in a way she hadn't experienced since high school. What did it feel like for her to be getting all this newfound attention from men on the street as she entered her mid-thirties? From her telling, pretty great! Why had she been hiding her beauty under a bushel all these years? As a single woman on the prowl, the attention to which she was suddenly subject was an important indicator of the fact that she'd been seriously underselling herself—inside and out—for a very long time.

Alongside a slight dose of discomfort, you may feel your emotions surrounding your clothing become suffused with a lightness and a joy you haven't felt since those high school days. Despite all of the struggles you have previously had with your clothing, you may rediscover a sense of fun. Once you remove the fit, color, and style challenges that have been dogging you all these years (along with the burdensome weight of all those nonworking garments you tossed out the door), a new sense of play may be available to you. Revel in it! The more fun you have, the more positive the messages your clothing will be transmitting. And this can only be a good thing, whether your personal-style mission statement revolves around adopting a more powerful presence or slithering into a sultrier look.

On a deeper level, you will certainly feel an increased sense of poise and self-confidence. An outfit you feel 100 percent proud of is an immeasurably powerful baseline with which to start your day. You will notice the difference the instant you step out of your door, and the benefits will only accrue throughout the days, weeks, and months that follow.

Now that you are in total control of what your clothing is saying, you have at your disposal a complete and powerful vocabulary that will enable you to change the arc of the conversation—the conversation that is the backdrop to your entire life. The story it tells from here on out is up to you.

Taking It to the Next Level: How to Become an Expert Shopper

Throughout this book, I've been focusing on ridding you of a fear of shopping and helping you into a more mindful, conscious, and confident state of being. But as you get more comfortable carving out your personal style as a style ninja who knows exactly what brands, fits, and colors to seek out, you'll find yourself naturally upping the ante. You will become that French woman with the highest of standards. And once you've rescued your wardrobe from a state of disarray, you'll want to adopt a few mind-sets that will allow you to make the most of your future acquisitions:

- Keep an eye out for your trouble spots. If you have difficulty fitting into pants, pants should always be in the back of your mind. Force yourself to try them on, even if it's not your favorite thing to do. And be open to surprises—you may have written off skinny jeans but find the one brand that fits you like a glove. But you'll never know unless you're willing to try them on for size.

- Always know what you are missing. Keeping a running to-do list will enable you to grab that necessary item when you spot it. Is your black cardigan starting to fray at the cuffs? It's on the list. Are your nude flats about to kick the bucket? Pay attention to this stuff, and don't forget about those Fashion Dares you committed to on page 218—also be on the lookout for those items that stretch your fashion muscles in unfamiliar ways.

- Pay attention to your fashion glitches. Life is full of ups and downs, and there will always be that morning when you can't quite seem to pull it together, that outfit you end up giving up on at the last minute because you just can't seem to make it work. Don't just move on—make a note to come back and evaluate the problem later on. Either a piece of that outfit needs to go, or a supplementary garment needs to be purchased, or a combination needs to be rethought. If those slightly baggier jeans make you feel unprofessional, perhaps they should be reserved for the weekend and paired with a slim-fitting tank top or tee or a deconstructed linen shirt.

■ **Find that boutique that makes you happy.** If you happen upon a store where everything feels like it was tailor-made for you, consider yourself lucky. Don't take your good fortune for granted—become a regular. Come back once a season to see what's new. Sign up for the store's newsletter so that you can keep abreast of sales. If the store is small enough that you can become a recognized VIP, you're likely to be the beneficiary of special treatment. Don't be surprised if you are treated to impromptu markdowns every once in a while.

■ **Shop with (and against) the seasons.** Though it's easy to write off seasonal shopping as a trick designed to entice you into stores several times a year, the fact is that clothing *is* disposable. It does need to be replaced, and an upcoming change of season is a helpful reminder that it's time to do just that. So when the seasons are about to change, take an inventory of your closet (more on that in a moment) and see what you're missing. That old trope about shopping against the seasons, of course, still holds true—that's when you get the benefit of those inventory-clearing deals.

- Hone your eye. As you become more and more conscious of your clothing and the message it communicates, you'll find yourself applying this heightened awareness to the world around you. One of my favorite things to do on a New York City subway is the thirty-second outfit scan. I can't help myself—when I look around at a crowd of strangers, what I see is style. Everything from great style to almost-there style to gouge-your-eyes-out terrible style. (Believe me, in the last case it takes all of my willpower *not* to speak up.) Soon, you, too, will join me in this useful and enjoyable pastime. Use your newfound awareness to mine those public spaces for style ideas. If a person looks terrific, try to analyze why that is so. Is her gray top playing off of her striking silver bob, popped by a pair of peach-colored jeans set off by a flowy long white cardigan? If someone looks almost great, can you identify the tweak that would have taken her outfit the distance? Feel free to silently judge, but also look to squeeze actionable information out of these brief encounters. Sometimes those magazine spreads are so otherworldly perfect that it can be difficult to grasp a real-life takeaway.

■ **Find a style icon.** Looking for real-life style inspiration? Forget about those celebrities running around half naked in numbers that have little to do with real life—look for a style icon closer to home. Is there a coworker whose outfits always make you swoon? A friend whose compositions put the rest of your crew to shame? An acquaintance you're always complimenting? Make this icon a mental touchstone. Next time you're in a store or in front of a mirror and you're feeling lost, you can just ask yourself: "Would Maisie wear this?" The answer should be immediately apparent.

Your Ever-Changing Closet

We are nearing the end of our journey together, and frankly, I'm a bit sad about that! But in a sense, this is only the beginning, because everything you are doing throughout this book—from the self-assessment exercises to the closet purge to the accumulation of quality and signature pieces—is going to become part of a life-long process.

No matter its level of quality, all clothing is ultimately disposable. All fabrics have an eventual expiration date, and so it is that our clothing must be continually replaced. Beyond that, our lives continually change in ways both expected and surprising. In order to keep up with these changes, you must treat your closet as a living, breathing organism. Care for your closet, and it will return the favor tenfold.

I've mentioned the notion of the biannual closet sweep several times, but as we approach the end of our time together I want to take a moment to reiterate the importance of this concept. Twice a year, every year, you should be combing through your wardrobe, using the process we outlined in Chapter 5 to assess which pieces are in need of refreshment, replacement, or disposal; refer back to the Seven Habits of Highly Effective Closets on page 187 as needed.

Go through this process as you are switching out your seasons. Even if your closet *does* have the room to accommodate your entire wardrobe, you'll want to move things around so that the current season is the most visible. And if you live in a seasonless paradise, please remember to sort through your stuff at least twice a year.

Outside of these biannual sweeps, you should be cycling items out of your wardrobe anytime you notice that a piece of clothing is past its prime or just not doing you any favors. And you should feel *great* about getting rid of stuff on a regular basis. When you excise this kind of clothing from your wardrobe, you aren't being wasteful—you are giving yourself a gift. Just like a responsible cook who makes sure her fridge and pantry aren't filled with decomposing produce, congealed leftovers, and the flavorless dust that used to resemble a spice, you are acting as the responsible owner of a happy and functional wardrobe. Congratulations!

Never Settle for Anything Less than a 10

If there's one thing we can count on in life, it's the occasional curveball. No matter how good your intentions, how strong your resolve, or how profound the transformation you enact by following the methods outlined in this book, there will be times in your life when you go through a slump—and that slump begins to express itself in the clothing you are wearing.

When these times come to pass, remember the tricks I've taught you. If you are down, reach for that bright and cheerful color with its magical mood-enhancing qualities.

If you can't deal with a face full of makeup, throw on a bright lipstick, pull your hair back in a ponytail, and call it a day. Remember the promises you have made to yourself. Turn back to the mission statement you wrote down in your little black book, and ask yourself whether you're doing right by it. Subject your everyday dress routine to the checklist outlined on pages 23 to 25.

Challenging yourself to up the ante even when you're at your lowest may seem like some kind of masochistic punishment, but it is *anything* but. Given the power of our clothing to influence our moods and thereby change our experience, dressing with consciousness is one of the best things we can do to pump ourselves up when we are feeling low.

Beware in general of falling back into those familiar comfort zones—the uniforms that don't necessarily look actively bad but don't do much for you, either. Always ask yourself whether you are presenting yourself as the perfect 10 that you are. If you feel yourself falling into a pattern of style doldrums, ask yourself why. What is making you want to hide out? Are you feeling self-conscious about something? Have you been taking care of yourself? Eating well, sleeping enough, getting enough exercise? Have you remembered to take time off? While a cute outfit and a happy dose of color can cure many ills, sometimes a girl just needs a break. (Be sure to revel in that break by wearing the most luxurious, comfortable, and flattering casuals and loungewear you can get your hands on.)

Above all else, remember the rule of the perfect 10—your ultimate goal is never to wear anything less. Why on earth *would* you, knowing what you now know?

Remember to Make Conscious Dressing a Daily Practice

One of my biggest goals in this book has been to get you to question the assumption that style is a switch you can turn on and off at will. This is how most people operate, and it's a recipe for a wardrobe that's full of holes and inconsistencies, for an underdeveloped aesthetic sense that leaves us grasping at straws on those occasions when we *do* try to pull ourselves together.

Practice makes perfect—but beyond that, and more important for our purposes, practice eventually *becomes* habit. Virtuosic violinists don't master their craft by cramming for performances the night before. They practice for hours a day, so that when they get up on that brightly lit stage in front of all those people, instinct takes over and their instrument takes on a life of its own. That is what I want for you.

As you've probably experienced, when you're not in the habit of eating healthfully, it seems incredibly difficult—but once you get into it and make it a daily practice, it's not such a big deal. This rule applies to everything in our lives. Mindful habits are just as sticky as bad habits. That's why when it comes to the way you dress, I'm going to ask you to be rigorous, and to make that rigor a daily practice. Interrogate your uniforms, interrogate your unconscious style habits.

At first, this will be challenging—but hopefully it will be an interesting challenge, and over time, it will become easier.

Have *Fun*!

I will leave you with one last bit of advice: Regardless of whether your overarching goal is to look more powerful or to ramp up the sex appeal, if you have more fun with your clothes, then we have succeeded! Try not to worry too much. Adopt a lighthearted, playful spirit when shopping and dressing. Don't be afraid to try on personas that don't feel 100 percent like you. Experiment! Turn your closet into a happy space, and that positive message will radiate out into the world.

As I've said, because a wardrobe needs to be continually refreshed over the years, this is going to be a lifelong process. So learn to love it. It's a part of life. Don't feel guilty about the time or money or care you expend on your clothing. You can't go naked—it's against the law. You are legally bound to buy and wear clothes. And they might as well be great. Just like you.

acknowledgments

Writing a book about self-discovery requires that I thank all the people who helped me on my own path of learning and exploring. I'd like to thank the teachers who opened my eyes and my heart to so much over the years—especially Patricia Moreno, who inspired me on the path of gratitude and mindfulness. I want to express my deep gratitude to my team at Simon & Schuster, Jen Bergstrom and Trish Boczkowski, for their encouragement and belief in me, and Elana Cohen, for keeping us all on track, my agent, Farley Chase, for his open heart, my co-author, Savannah Ashour, for her patience and wisdom, and my friends, designer Rolando Santana, for his wonderful work and talent, makeup artist Amanda Thesen, for her expertise, and Andrea Mitchell, who was my guardian angel on this project from the very start. I want to thank all my friends who love and support me unconditionally . . . you know who you are! And finally, I want to thank my John, who loves me like no one else ever has, and my family, especially my mom, who has taught me everything I know about style and fashion, and most important, how to discover and embrace who you really are.